# MEDITERRANEAN DIET COOKBOOK

1600 Days of Easy & Affordable Recipes for Beginners
with 25 Weeks Simple Flexible Meal Plan to Kickstart
a New Healthy life

**CAMILA WHITE**

# TABLE OF CONTENT

# INTRODUCTION

The Mediterranean Diet has taken the world by storm, and it's easy to see why: It provides its practitioners with an easy-to-follow, healthy diet plan and gives them access to foods and spices they may not have otherwise been exposed to.

The Mediterranean diet is a traditional eating pattern in countries bordering the Mediterranean Sea. It's based on the traditional eating habits of people living in Greece, Italy, Spain, and Southern France, where life expectancy rates are among the highest in the world.

The Mediterranean diet has become one of the most popular diets in the world, and with good reason – it's tasty, healthy, and easy to follow. The typical Mediterranean diet consists of fish, whole grains, fresh produce, legumes, nuts, and other foods high in vitamins and antioxidants but low in salt and unhealthy fats.

Fish and seafood are consumed in moderate amounts, while poultry, eggs, cheese, and yogurt are eaten in smaller quantities. Red meat is eaten only occasionally.

Olive oil is the main source of fat. It's used for cooking and preparing dressings for salads. The consumption of olive oil has been shown to help maintain a healthy heart. Red wine is typically consumed with meals but not during pregnancy or breastfeeding. Dairy products contain natural sugars, so they should also be limited, although full-fat dairy products provide valuable nutrients such as calcium, Protein, and vitamin D.

A typical day's breakfast might consist of oatmeal with fruit and a cup of coffee or tea. Lunch would likely be a salad made up of greens, tomatoes, cucumbers, onions, olives, and other veggies topped with two tablespoons of balsamic vinegar dressing. Dinner might consist of fish topped with broccoli and garlic roasted olive oil.

Did you know that the Mediterranean diet is one of the world's healthiest diets, proven to reduce your risk of heart disease, diabetes, cancer, and Alzheimer's?

In addition to being delicious, this diet is said to protect against various illnesses, including cancer and Alzheimer's disease. It is worth noting that many people find the Mediterranean diet easier to stick to long-term when it includes occasional red meat intake instead of excluding all animal products entirely.

One study showed reduced mortality rates among participants who followed a Mediterranean diet compared to participants who followed more Westernized diets. This study's results suggest it could be related to better management of chronic health conditions like type 2 diabetes, hypertension, and elevated cholesterol.

While we don't know for sure, it seems plausible that following a Mediterranean diet rich in fruits, vegetables, beans, and whole grains is healthier than following more Westernized diets rich in processed foods.

Follow our step-by-step guide to introducing yourself to this revolutionary way of eating that allows you to cut out processed foods while enjoying fresh produce, grains, and legumes.

# CHAPTER ONE

## THE MEDITERRANEAN DIET – A HEALTHY AND DELICIOUS WAY OF EATING

### *What is the Mediterranean Diet?*

The Mediterranean diet is a traditional way of eating in countries bordering the Mediterranean Sea. The diet emphasizes mostly plant-based foods, including vegetables, fruits, whole grains, legumes, nuts, and seeds.

Olive oil is the primary fat source, and fish and poultry are eaten moderately. Dairy products, red meat, and processed foods are eaten only occasionally. Oils such as canola, soybean, corn, sunflower, and peanut oils are not included on the list of healthy fats because they lack nutrients. Moderate alcohol consumption (one glass for women and two for men) is also part of this healthy lifestyle.

The popularity of this diet has been growing in recent years due to its emphasis on fresh food over convenience food. It has been linked to lower rates of heart disease, diabetes, cancer, and obesity because it's low in saturated fats but high in omega-3 fatty acids from fish which help reduce inflammation.

In addition, those who adhere to this diet tend to have lower levels of bad LDL cholesterol and higher levels of good HDL cholesterol. They also have lower triglyceride levels. While some diets may be too restrictive or hard to maintain, the Mediterranean diet is easy to follow since there are many variations of this eating style.

There are so many delicious foods that one could eat while following this diet: veggies, fruit, beans, and lentils, bread and cereals made with whole grain flour, or pasta with tomato sauce.

# 6 Health Benefits of the Mediterranean Diet

The Mediterranean diet offers lots of amazing benefits, seven of which we'll discuss below:

1. The Mediterranean diet has been shown to reduce the risk of heart disease:
This benefit is seen with virtually any form of dietary pattern shown to have favorable effects on blood cholesterol levels. This is thought to be partially due to an increase in beneficial HDL cholesterol levels, along with a decrease in harmful LDL cholesterol and triglyceride levels.
The studies often linked to finding these results tend to be cross-sectional rather than longitudinal, so we can't definitively say whether it was due to their diets or not.

2. The diet can help lower cholesterol and blood pressure levels:
Cholesterol levels are lowered when following this eating plan because there is less consumption of saturated fats and more unsaturated fats from plants. In addition, salt intake decreases when following this diet, lowering blood pressure.
However, recent research suggests that replacing animal Proteins with plant Proteins does not necessarily lead to a better lipid profile. Therefore, it may be necessary to combine strategies such as reducing animal Protein intake while increasing vegetable intake to lower bad cholesterol levels.

3. The diet can help improve blood sugar control in people with diabetes:
Several reviews have found that the Mediterranean diet helps manage type 2 diabetes mellitus. For example, one study found that type 2 diabetics who followed the diet had significantly improved glycemic control and needed less medication over time.

Furthermore, those who follow the traditional Mediterranean diet fare better at controlling weight gain caused by insulin resistance by restricting carbohydrates to higher amounts like whole grains or potatoes, which contain lots of carbohydrates.

A major factor contributing to decreased insulin resistance could be reduced calorie intake since individuals consuming this type of food produce smaller portions and thus consume fewer calories overall compared to typical Western diets.

Finally, olive oil appears to slow stomach emptying, which leads to delayed gastric emptying and thus helps improve glucose tolerance.


4. The diet may help reduce the risk of Alzheimer's disease and other forms of dementia:

There is evidence that the Mediterranean diet may be protective against age-related cognitive decline. A 2011 study looked at lifestyle factors and cognitive function in a group of healthy adults and found that those with the most Mediterranean lifestyles, meaning they ate foods typically consumed on this diet, had the lowest scores on tests measuring mental abilities.

These associations were stronger in older adults because of their closer adherence to the Mediterranean diet. Other potential reasons for a protective effect include the high levels of antioxidant compounds and vitamins found in this eating, which can reduce oxidative stress and inflammation throughout the body.


5. The diet is also associated with a lower risk of Parkinson's disease:

While research on Parkinson's disease is ongoing, early studies suggest that eating more foods typical of a Mediterranean diet may help prevent or delay some age-related mental decline.

What exactly in these foods affects your risk for neurodegenerative diseases isn't clear yet. However, it seems likely that a combination of antioxidants and vitamins found in fruits, vegetables, legumes, cereals (like whole grains), beans, and fish are protective against age-related mental decline since these types of food are all linked to lower inflammation levels.

6. It can improve overall sleep patterns:
Studies suggest that in addition to improving cholesterol levels, weight, blood pressure, and cardiovascular health in general, following a Mediterranean diet can improve overall sleep patterns.
Research looking at participants following a traditional Mediterranean diet has found an improvement in their sleeping patterns.

# The Mediterranean Food Pyramid

The basis of the Mediterranean diet is plants – lots of fruits and vegetables, whole grains, legumes, and nuts. Olive oil is used in place of other fats, and there is moderate consumption of fish, poultry, eggs, dairy, and red wine.

This way of eating has been shown to have numerous health benefits, including reducing the risk of heart disease, stroke, cancer, and Alzheimer's disease. Plus, it's delicious!

So if you want to improve your health and enjoy delicious food simultaneously, the Mediterranean diet is a great option. It can be easy to follow but does require some preparation.

The foundation of this diet is plant-based foods like fruit, vegetables, whole grains, and beans which provide fiber and vitamins. Red meat is limited and replaced with alternatives like white meat or poultry. There's also a moderate intake of cheese, yogurt, eggs, and other Protein sources, along with plenty of healthy fats from olive oil or avocado. Finally, of course, you can drink alcohol in moderation as well (though not more than one glass per day for women).

# But where do you start?

**Foods to eat:**

Vegetables and Fruits: Vegetables should make up 50% of what you eat daily, so if you're going to cook veggies, make sure they're cooked properly by steaming them for 20 minutes until they are just tender. Canned vegetables should only be eaten occasionally because they often contain added salt and preservatives that aren't good for us.

Fruits should make up about 25% of what we eat each day so look out for ways to add fresh fruit into every meal – having fresh grapes available when making salads is an easy way to get started.

Whole Grains: These are important because they help regulate blood sugar levels, lower cholesterol levels, reduce inflammation, and may even protect against certain cancers such as colon cancer. To include these in your diet, replace refined grain products like white bread with whole grain options. Other good choices include brown rice, oatmeal, barley, and quinoa.

Legumes: Beans are another carbohydrate that you should regularly include because they offer many health benefits, including increased satiety and reduced hunger cravings later in the day due to their high fiber content. If you don't think you'll enjoy these enough, try adding them to soups or stews or tossing them over pasta instead of traditional spaghetti sauce. Try to incorporate 3 cups of beans, lentils, or peas each week.

Nuts and Seeds: Finally, nuts and seeds are an excellent source of Protein and unsaturated fat, promoting weight loss. They're high in calories, so be careful not to go overboard, but a handful is generally recommended. Choose raw almonds, walnuts, pumpkin seeds, sunflower seeds, and flaxseeds.

**Foods to eat in moderation:**

Cheese: Cheese is another way to get Protein and calcium, so you should include it as long as you limit your portions to no more than six ounces per day.

Yogurt: If you enjoy dairy foods, yogurt is the best option because of its high probiotic content, which helps maintain gut health.

Eggs: Eggs are perfect for breakfast because they're packed with Protein and omega-3 fatty acids, making you less hungry throughout the day. Eggs are a great meat substitute if you want to keep the Mediterranean diet more vegetarian.

Olive Oil: This is a mainstay of the Mediterranean diet because of its health benefits and should be used in moderation as cooking oil and dressing. If you're following a strict Mediterranean diet, use light olive oil because it has fewer calories than regular olive oil.

Wine: This can be enjoyed in moderation with one drink per day for women and two drinks per day for men. It's important to remember that red wine is high in resveratrol which has been shown to have anti-aging properties, and some studies have shown that it may even improve heart health. The best time to drink alcohol is during a meal because it helps slow down digestion and prevents blood sugar spikes. Choose mixed drinks over hard liquor because they don't contain as many empty calories and artificial ingredients.

**Foods to avoid:**

Processed Meats: Processed meats include deli meats, bacon, ham, hot dogs, and sausages. These meats often come with nitrates which are preservatives linked to cancer risk. These meats also contain lots of sodium which can increase blood pressure levels and should be avoided if you already have hypertension or diabetes.

Pastries and Sweets: Pastries are made with white flour, which means they're higher in carbs than healthier options like whole wheat bread. The gluten found in pastries can cause inflammation which leads to digestive problems and weight gain.

Chocolate and Candy: These sweets might taste good, but their high sugar content will lead to weight gain and increase the risk of Type 2 Diabetes.

Fruit Juices: Fruit juices are very concentrated sources of sugar and carbohydrates, so try drinking them in moderation (half a cup at most). You're better off eating fresh fruit or making your juice at home.

Processed Foods: When it comes to junk food, the Mediterranean diet takes a stricter stance. This is because they're high in fat and salt, which contribute to various serious diseases, including cardiovascular disease, certain cancers, and Type 2 Diabetes.

Sugar: Sugars are still a large part of the modern diet and should be limited because they can raise blood glucose levels, leading to insulin resistance.

Extra Virgin Olive Oil: An Essential Part of the Mediterranean Diet

Extra virgin olive oil is the cornerstone of the Mediterranean diet. This healthy, flavorful oil is packed with monounsaturated fats and antioxidants, making it a heart-healthy choice for cooking and dressing. Unlike other oils that are high in polyunsaturated fats, extra virgin olive oil can withstand higher heat without oxidizing and turning into trans fats.

The three key things to look for when buying extra virgin olive oil are country of origin (some countries produce better quality oils than others), color (the lighter the color, the less time it's been aged), and aroma (it should have a mild fruity smell).

# CHAPTER TWO

## EASY STEPS TO START YOUR JOURNEY TO A HEALTHY AND DELICIOUS MEDITERRANEAN DIET

The Mediterranean diet includes many of the world's healthiest foods, like fruits, vegetables, whole grains, nuts, and olive oil. Eating this way can reduce your risk of heart disease, stroke, and diabetes. Plus, those who follow this eating plan may have better moods and lower rates of depression than those who don't.

The Mediterranean diet has long been known as one of the healthiest and most nutritious ways to eat in the world, but despite its broad popularity, it isn't easy to figure out how to get started on it.

This guide will help you understand what it takes to start eating like people from countries surrounding the Mediterranean Sea and give you the tools you need to create your own healthy Mediterranean diet plan that works with your lifestyle and schedule.

1) Step away from Sugar

Sugar is one of the biggest enemies of a healthy diet. Not only is it loaded with empty calories, but it can also lead to cravings and overeating. If you're serious about eating healthy, you must cut sugar from your diet.

Get rid of all the sugary snacks and drinks in your house, such as candy, cookies, cake, soda, and fruit juice. They'll just tempt you or others who live with you, and it's best not to have them around at all. When shopping for groceries, read labels carefully and avoid anything with added sugars listed as one of the first five ingredients. Also, try looking for foods labeled with no added sugar on the label if you want something sweet now and then. It might take a while to kick your craving for sweets, but eventually, it will go away as long as you avoid things like ice cream containing high amounts of added sugars.

## 2) Add in more natural fats

The ketogenic diet is a high-fat, low-carbohydrate diet that has been shown to promote weight loss and improve overall health. The Mediterranean diet is a variation of the ketogenic diet that includes more natural fats, such as olive oil, nuts, and avocados.

Olive oil contains healthy fat in the form of oleic acid, which can reduce cholesterol levels in your blood. Nuts are also high in healthy fat and Protein, which can keep you feeling full longer while providing necessary nutrients for your body.

Avocados are another rich source of healthy fat that have other heart-healthy benefits like lowering cholesterol levels and reducing inflammation.

## 3) Eat plenty of whole grains

Eating plenty of whole grains is one of the most important aspects of a healthy Mediterranean diet. Not only are whole grains nutritious, but they can also help reduce the risk of heart disease and other chronic conditions.

Here are some tips for incorporating more whole grains into your diet:
- Stick with brown rice instead of white rice
- Eat rye bread instead of wheat bread
- Try quinoa instead of pasta or rice
- Try barley instead of potatoes or corn on the cob
- Make couscous out of whole wheat flour instead of white flour
- Take a second look at beans, lentils, and legumes such as chickpeas (aka garbanzo beans)
- Fill up on oats by making oatmeal in the morning or adding them to recipes during the day

## 4) Choose nutrient-dense vegetables

When starting a healthy Mediterranean diet, there are so many nutrient-dense vegetables to choose from. Vegetables like kale, spinach, Swiss chard, and collard greens are all excellent choices.

These leafy greens are packed with vitamins, minerals, and antioxidants.

Another great option is cruciferous vegetables like broccoli, Brussels sprouts, and cauliflower. These veggies are also full of nutrients and can help boost your immune system. Lastly, don't forget starchy vegetables like sweet potatoes and winter squash. These foods can help you feel fuller longer and are a great source of complex carbohydrates.

## 5) Eat well-rounded fish

The benefits of eating fish are plenty—it's a great source of lean protein, low in calories, and rich in omega-3 fatty acids, which are great for your heart. But with so many different types of fish out there, it can be tough to know where to start.

Luckily, the Mediterranean diet has you covered. This way of eating includes a variety of well-rounded fish that are perfect for beginners.

## 6) Cut back on processed meats

The first step is to cut back on processed meats. These are typically high in unhealthy fats and sodium, contributing to high blood pressure and other health problems. Instead, focus on eating more whole, unprocessed foods like fruits, vegetables, and lean protein sources. You should also make sure to get plenty of healthy fats from olive oil, nuts, and seeds.

## 7) Limit red meat intake

The first step is to cut back on your intake of red meat. Studies have shown that consuming large amounts of red meat can increase your risk of heart disease, cancer, and other chronic illnesses. Instead, try replacing red meat with chicken, fish, or tofu a few times per week.

You can also add more beans, legumes, and whole grains to your diet. These healthy choices will help you reduce your risk of chronic disease and improve your overall health. Please consult your physician if you would like assistance in making these changes, please consult your physician.

## 8) Have lots of poultry and eggs

One of the best things about the Mediterranean diet is that it allows for plenty of poultry and eggs. Poultry and eggs are packed with Protein and other essential nutrients for a healthy diet. And they're relatively low in calories, making them a great choice for those looking to lose weight.

As long as you don't overdo it, these two items can easily be incorporated into your daily diet without much hassle at all. Another thing to note is that both foods can be consumed at any part of the day, including breakfast.

## 9) Give up processed foods

If you're used to eating a lot of processed foods, making the switch to a healthy Mediterranean diet can seem daunting. But it's worth it! processed foods are loaded with unhealthy ingredients that can contribute to weight gain, heart disease, and other chronic health problems. Plus, they're often devoid of the nutrients your body needs to function properly. So ditching them is a smart move for your health.

10) Add seafood to your diet at least twice every week

Adding seafood to your diet is a great way to get started on a healthy Mediterranean diet. Seafood is packed with nutrients and healthy fats that are essential for a healthy body and mind. Plus, it's easy to find seafood that is sustainable and delicious. Here are some tips for getting started

11) Eat lots of fruits

One of the best things about the Mediterranean diet is that it emphasizes eating lots of fruits. Not only are these foods packed with nutrients, but they also help fill you up so you don't end up overeating. Aim to fill half your plate with veggies and fruit at every meal.

12) Stay hydrated and full with water, tea, coffee, and juice (In moderation!)

You can't go wrong by starting your day with a big glass of water. Drinking tea, coffee, and juice throughout the day will also help you stay hydrated and full. Just be sure to drink them in moderation so you don't consume too much sugar.

It's okay to indulge occasionally but make sure not to rely on these drinks as a way to start your day or keep yourself full.

13) Shop in specialty food stores or farmers' markets

If you want to get the most authentic and delicious Mediterranean foods, your best bet is to shop in specialty food stores or farmers' markets. This way, you can find unique items that you may not be able to find at a regular grocery store. Plus, you'll be supporting local businesses! Here are a few tips for shopping at these types of stores

# CHAPTER THREE

# BEANS & GRAINS

## *Tomato Rice*

Preparation time: 10 minutes; Cooking time: 25 minutes; Serves: 3
Ingredients:

- ¾ tsp. of fine sea salt
- 1 cup of uncooked medium-grain rice
- 1 garlic clove (finely chopped)
- 1 lb. (454 g) of canned crushed tomatoes, or 1 lb. (454 g) of fresh tomatoes (puréed inside a food processor)
- 1 medium onion (any variety) (chopped)
- 1 tbsp. of tomato paste
- 1 tsp. of granulated sugar
- 2 cups of hot water
- 2 tbsps. of chopped fresh mint or basil
- 2 tbsps. of extra virgin olive oil

Preparation:

1.     Pour the olive oil into a deep, wide pan to heat on medium heat. When it starts shimmering, include the onion and let it sauté for 3 to 4 minutes or till it softens. Afterward, add the garlic to the sauté for extra 30 seconds.

2.     Put the rice inside the pan and stir until the oil coats it very well. Stir in the tomato paste. Stir quickly then add the tomatoes, sugar, and sea salt. Stir.

3.     Pour the hot water into the pan, stir, then decrease the heat to low. Leave it covered and simmer for up to 20 minutes or just until the rice softens. (If the rice isn't soft enough, add a little more hot water and keep on cooking.) Take the pan off the heat.

4.    Put the mint or basil inside the pan and allow the rice to sit for about 10 minutes before you serve. To store, cover and refrigerate for a maximum of 4 days.

**Nutritional Information per Serving:**
Calories: 359, carbs: 60g, fat: 11g, fiber: 6g, Protein: 7g, sodium: 607mg

## *Sweet Potato and Chickpea Moroccan Stew*

Preparation time: 10 minutes; Cooking time: 40 minutes; Serves: 4
Ingredients:
- ½ lb. (227 g) of butternut squash (peeled & cut into ½-inch cubes)
- ½ tsp. of ground turmeric
- ½ tsp. of smoked paprika
- 1 cinnamon stick
- 1 tsp. of ground coriander
- 1 tsp. of ground cumin
- 2 medium red/white onions (finely chopped)
- 2 medium sweet potatoes (peeled & cut into ½-inch cubes)
- 3 medium carrots (around 8 oz. or 227 g) (peeled & cubed)
- 4 oz. (113 g) of prunes (pitted)
- 4 tomatoes (any variety) (chopped), or 20 oz. (567 g) of canned tomatoes (chopped)
- 6 garlic cloves (minced)
- 6 tbsps. of extra virgin olive oil
- 14 oz. (397 g) of canned chickpeas
- 14 oz. (397 g) of vegetable broth
- For serving: ½ cup of fresh parsley (chopped)

Preparation:

1.     Heat the olive oil inside a deep pan placed over medium heat. Once the oil starts to shimmer, put the onions inside the oil to sauté for around 5 minutes. Afterward, add the carrots and garlic. Sauté for just a minute.

2.     Add the coriander, cumin, paprika, cinnamon stick, and turmeric. Keep cooking, stirring constantly, for a minute. Add the sweet potatoes, squash, vegetable broth, tomatoes, and prunes. Stir and cover, then lessen to low heat and allow to simmer for about 20 minutes, stirring irregularly and simultaneously checking the water levels, till the vegetables are thoroughly cooked. (If the stew looks like it is drying out, add little hot water until the stew thickens.)

3.     Put the chickpeas into the pan and stir. Keep simmering for an additional 10 minutes, and add more water if needed. Take the pan off the heat, get rid of the cinnamon stick, then leave the stew to cool for about 10 minutes.

4.     When all is set to serve, sprinkle the top of the stew with chopped parsley and refrigerate for as much as 4 days.

**Nutritional Information per Serving:**
Calories: 471, carbs: 63g, fat: 23g, fiber: 12g, Protein: 9g, sodium: 651mg

# Lentil & Zucchini Boats

Preparation time: 15 minutes, Cooking time: 50 minutes, Serves: 4

Ingredients:

- ¼ cup of chopped fresh flat-leaf parsley
- ¼ tsp. of crushed red pepper flakes
- ¼ tsp. of salt
- ½ cup of shredded part-skim mozzarella cheese
- ½ medium red onion (peeled & diced)
- 1 clove of garlic (peeled & minced)
- 1 cup of dried green lentils (rinsed & drained)
- 1 cup of marinara sauce
- 1 tbsp. of olive oil
- 2 cups of water
- 4 medium zucchini (trimmed & cut lengthwise)

Preparation:

1.    Get an Instant Pot® and put the lentils, water, and salt in it. Shut the lid and set the steam release on Sealing. Press the Manual and set the time to 12 minutes. As soon as the timer beeps, quick release of the pressure till the pot's float valve drops. Press Cancel, take off the lid, then drain any excess liquid. Move the lentils into a medium bowl and then set them aside.

2.    Press Sauté and heat the oil. Add the onion and cook for around 3 minutes or until it becomes tender. Add the garlic and cook for around 30 seconds or until fragrant. Add the marinara sauce and the crushed red pepper flakes. Stir to mix then press Cancel. Stir in the lentils.

3.    Let the oven preheat to 350ºF or (180ºC and spray nonstick cooking spray on a 9" by 13" baking dish.

4.    Use a teaspoon to hollow out each of the zucchini halves. Place the zucchini in the prepared baking dish. Then divide the lentil mixture among the prepared zucchini and top with the cheese. Let it bake for 30 to 35 minutes, or just until the zucchini gets tender and cheese melts and browns. Use parsley as a topping and serve while it's still hot.

## Nutritional Information per Serving:
Calories: 326, carbs: 39g, fat: 10g, fiber: 16g, Protein: 22g, sodium: 568mg

### *Creamy Yellow Lentil Soup*
Preparation time: 15 minutes, Cooking time: 20 minutes, Serves: 6
Ingredients:
- ¼ tsp. of salt
- ½ tsp. of ground black pepper
- 1 medium carrot (peeled & chopped)
- 1 medium yellow onion (peeled & chopped)
- 1 tsp. of ground cumin
- 2 cloves garlic (peeled & minced)
- 2 cups of dried yellow lentils (rinsed & drained)
- 2 tbsps. of olive oil
- 6 cups of water

Preparation:
1.    Pour oil inside the Instant Pot® and press the Sauté button. When it heats, add the carrot and onion. Cook for about 3 minutes until tender. Add cumin, garlic, salt, and pepper. Cook for about 30 seconds until it gets fragrant, then press Cancel.

2.    Add the lentils and water to the pot, close the lid, set the steam release to Sealing, then press Manual, and set the time to 15 minutes. As soon as the timer beeps, naturally release the pressure for around 15 minutes.

3.    Take off the lid and use an immersion blender to purée or place them into a blender in batches.

4.    Serve warm.

**Nutritional Information per Serving:**
Calories: 248, carbs: 35g, fat: 5g, fiber: 8g, Protein: 15g, sodium: 118mg

## Brown Rice with Apricots, Cherries, and Toasted Pecans

Preparation time: 10 minutes, Cooking time: 55 minutes, Serves: 2
Ingredients:

- 2 tbsps. of olive oil
- 2 green onions (sliced)
- ½ cup of brown rice
- 1 cup of chicken stock
- 4 to 5 dried apricots (chopped)
- 2 tbsps. of dried cherries
- 2 tbsps. of pecans (toasted & chopped)
- Sea salt
- Freshly ground pepper (to taste)

Preparation:

1.    Pour the olive oil into a medium saucepan to heat and put the green onions into it.

2.    Let it sauté for 1 to 2 minutes before adding the rice. Stir well to coat in the oil and add the stock.

3.    Let it boil then reduce the heat. Cover and simmer for about 50 minutes.

4.    Take off the lid, then add the pecans, apricots, and cherries. Cover for extra 10 minutes.

5.    Use a fork to fluff then mix the fruit in the rice. Use the freshly ground pepper and sea salt to season. Serve.

**Nutritional Information per Serving:**
Calories: 429, carbs: 54g, fat: 21g, fiber: 4g, Protein: 8g, sodium: 43mg

# Moroccan Vegetables & Chickpeas

Preparation time: 25 minutes, Cooking time: 6 hours, Serves: 6
Ingredients:

- ¼ cup of diced dried apricots
- ¼ cup of diced dried figs
- ¼ tsp. of ground red pepper
- 1 (15-oz. / 425-g) can of diced tomatoes (with the juice)
- 1 cup of plain Greek yogurt
- 1 large bell pepper of any color (chopped)
- 1 large carrot (cut into ¼-inch rounds)
- 1 large yellow onion (chopped)
- 1 tbsp. of ground coriander
- 1 tsp. of fresh ginger (peeled & grated)
- 1 tsp. of ground cumin
- 1¾ cups of vegetable stock
- 2 garlic cloves (minced)
- 2 large baking potatoes (peeled & cubed)
- 3 cups of canned chickpeas (rinsed & drained)
- 6 oz. (170 g) of green beans (trimmed & cut into bite-size pieces)
- 8 oz. (227 g) of fresh baby spinach
- Black pepper
- Sea salt

Preparation:
1.    Place the potatoes, carrot, bell pepper, onion, green beans, ginger, and garlic inside a slow cooker. Stir in the chickpeas, diced tomatoes, and vegetable stock. Then sprinkle cumin, coriander, black pepper, red pepper, and salt over it.

2.    Cover with the lid and cook for 6 hours on high or until the veggies get tender.

3.　　Add the apricots, spinach, Greek yogurt, and figs. Cook for about 4 minutes, stirring simultaneously till the spinach wilts.

4.　　Serve hot.


**Nutritional Information per Serving:**
Calories: 307, carbs: 57g, fat: 5g, fiber: 12g, Protein: 13g, sodium: 513mg


### *Baked Farro Risotto with Sage*

Preparation time: 5 minutes, Cooking time: 35 minutes, Serves 6
Ingredients:
- ½ tsp. of salt
- 1 cup of Parmesan cheese (grated & divided)
- 1 cup of tomato sauce
- 1 tbsp. of fresh sage (chopped)
- 1 yellow onion (diced)
- 1½ cups of uncooked farro
- 2 tbsps. of olive oil
- 2½ cups of chicken broth
- 3 garlic cloves (minced)
- Olive oil cooking spray

Preparation:
1.　　Let the air fryer preheat to 380ºF or 193ºC. Get a 5-cup capacity casserole dish and use olive oil cooking spray to coat the inside lightly (The casserole dish's shape will depend on the air fryer's size, but it should hold a minimum of 5 cups.)

2.　　Mix the farro, tomato sauce, broth, sage, onion, garlic, salt, ½ cup of Parmesan, and olive oil inside a big bowl.

3.     Pour the mixture into the ready casserole dish and use aluminum foil to cover it.

4.     Let it bake for 20 minutes before removing the cover. Stir and sprinkle the leftover ½ cup of Parmesan on top. Bake for extra 15 minutes.

5.     Stir properly and serve.


**Nutritional Information per Serving:**
Calories: 227, carbs: 27g, fat: 11.3g, fiber: 3.4g, Protein: 7.3g, sodium: 889mg


## *Savory Gigantes Plaki (Baked Giant White Beans)*
Preparation time: 5 minutes, Cooking time: 30 minutes, Serves: 4

Ingredients:
- ¼ cup of fresh parsley (chopped)
- ¼ cup of olive oil
- ½ tbsp. of tomato paste
- ½ tsp. of salt
- ½ yellow onion (diced)
- 1 (15-oz. / 425g) can of cooked butter beans (drained & rinsed)
- 1 cup of diced fresh tomatoes
- 2 garlic cloves (minced)
- Olive oil cooking spray

Preparation:

1.     Let the air fryer preheat to 380ºF or 193ºC. Get a 5-cup capacity casserole dish and use olive oil cooking spray to coat the inside lightly (The casserole dish's shape will depend on the air fryer's size, but it should hold a minimum of 5 cups.)

2.     Mix the tomatoes, tomato paste, butter beans, onion, garlic, olive oil, and salt inside a big bowl until well combined.

3.     Pour the tomato mixture into the primed casserole dish then use the chopped parsley as a topping.

4.     Place it in the air fryer to bake for 15 minutes. Stir properly and return it to the air fryer to bake for additional 15 minutes.

**Nutritional Information per Serving:**
Calories: 199, carbs: 8g, fat: 18..6g, fiber: 3g, Protein: 2g, sodium: 300mg

### *Greek Baked Beans*

Preparation time: 5 minutes, Cooking time: 30 minutes, Serves: 4

Ingredients:
- ¼ cup of olive oil
- ½ tsp. of black pepper
- ½ tsp. of salt
- ½ yellow onion (diced)
- 1 (15-oz. / 425-g) can of cannellini beans (drained & rinsed)
- 1 (15-oz. / 425-g) can of great northern beans (drained & rinsed)
- 1 (8-oz. / 227-g) can of tomato sauce
- 1 bay leaf
- 1 tbsp. of balsamic vinegar

- 1½ tbsp. of raw honey
- 2 garlic cloves (minced)
- 2 oz. (57 g) of feta cheese (crumbled), for serving
- 2 tbsps. of chopped fresh dill
- Olive oil cooking spray

Preparation:

1.    Let the air fryer preheat to 360ºF or 182ºC. Get a 5-cup capacity casserole dish and use olive oil cooking spray to coat the inside lightly (The casserole dish's shape will depend on the air fryer's size, but it should hold a minimum of 5 cups.)

2.    Mix all the ingredients apart from the feta cheese inside a big bowl. Stir to combine properly.

3.    Pour the mixture into the primed casserole dish.

4.    Place it in the air fryer to bake for 30 minutes.

5.    Get it out of the air fryer and get rid of the bay leaf. Sprinkle the top with the crumbled feta and serve.

**Nutritional Information per Serving:**
Calories: 336, carbs: 34g, fat: 19g, fiber: 9.4g, Protein: 11g, sodium: 497mg

# *Spanish Rice*

Preparation time: 10 minutes, Cooking time: 20 minutes, Serves: 4

Ingredients:
- 1 large tomato (finely diced)
- 1 medium onion (finely chopped)
- 1 tsp. of salt
- 1 tsp. of smoked paprika
- 1½ cups of basmati rice
- 2 tbsps. of extra-virgin olive oil
- 2 tbsps. of tomato paste
- 3 cups of water

Preparation:
1.    Put the olive oil, tomato, and onion inside a medium pot placed on medium heat, and cook for 3 minutes.

2.    While stirring, add the tomato paste, salt, paprika, and rice. Let it cook for a minute.

3.    Pour in the water then cover the pot and reduce to low heat. Cook for about 12 minutes.

4.    Toss the rice gently then cover, it again and cook for additional 3 minutes.

**Nutritional Information per Serving:**
Calories: 328, carbs: 60g, fat: 7g, fiber: 2g, Protein: 6g, sodium: 651mg

# CHAPTER FOUR

# BEEF, PORK, & LAMB

## *Herb-Marinated Grilled Lamb Loin Chops*

Preparation time: 5 minutes, Cooking time: 10 - 12 minutes, Serves: 4 – 6

Ingredients:
- ½ cup of fresh cilantro or parsley (finely chopped)
- 1 cup of fresh mint (finely chopped)
- 2 scallions or green onions (finely chopped)
- 2 tbsps. of pomegranate molasses
- 3 tbsps. of olive oil
- 6 lamb loin chops
- Freshly ground black pepper (to taste)
- Zest & juice of 1 lemon

Preparation:
1.    Put the olive oil, lemon juice, lemon zest, mint, pomegranate molasses, scallions, and parsley together inside a small bowl and whisk until properly combined.

2.    Place the lamb inside a large-sized zip-top plastic bag. Put the marinade and seal the bag. Massage the marinade to cover all the sides of the chops. Place it in a fridge for a minimum of 1 hour or overnight.

3.    When you're ready to cook, set a grill to heat on medium.

4.    Get the chops out of the marinade before discarding the marinade. Use pepper to season to taste. Then grill the chops for about

10-12 minutes, turning one time, for medium. Allow it to rest for about 10 minutes before you serve.

**Nutritional Information per Serving:**
Calories: 182, carbs: 10g, fat: 11g, fiber: 0g, Protein: 10g, sodium: 46mg

## *Pork and Cabbage Egg Roll in a Bowl*

Preparation time: 10 minutes, Cooking time: 10 minutes, Serves: 6

Ingredients:
- ¼ cup of low-sodium chicken broth
- 1 clove of garlic (peeled & minced)
- 1 lb. (454 g) of ground pork
- 1 medium yellow onion (peeled & chopped)
- 1 tbsp. of light olive oil
- 1 tsp. of garlic chili sauce
- 1 tsp. of sesame oil
- 2 (10-oz. / 283-g) bags of shredded coleslaw mix
- 2 tbsps. of soy sauce
- 2 tsps. of fresh ginger (minced)

Preparation:
1.     Pour the olive oil into the Instant Pot® and press Sauté to heat it. Include the pork and sauté for about 8 minutes or until it is cooked through. Add the onion, ginger, and garlic then cook for about 2 minutes or until fragrant. Stir in the soy sauce and chicken broth then press Cancel.

2.     Spread the coleslaw mix on the pork without mixing them, and then shut the lid. Set the steam release to Sealing, press Manual, then set the time to 0 minutes.

3.    Do a quick release of the pressure when the timer beeps and let the float valve drop before opening the lid. Stir in the garlic chili sauce and sesame oil.

4.    Serve hot.

**Nutritional Information per Serving:**
Calories: 283, carbs: 5g, fat: 24g, fiber: 2g, Protein: 12g, sodium: 507mg

# Spaghetti with Meaty Mushroom Sauce

Preparation time: 15 minutes, Cooking time: 23 minutes, Serves: 6

Ingredients:
- ½ lb. (227 g) of 90 percent lean ground beef
- ½ tsp. of ground fennel
- 1 (14½-oz. / 411-g) can of fire-roasted tomatoes (drained)
- 1 (25-oz. / 709-g) jar of marinara sauce
- 1 clove of garlic (peeled & minced)
- 1 cup of grated Parmesan cheese
- 1 lb. (454 g) of sliced crimini mushrooms
- 1 lb. (454 g) of spaghetti (broken in half)
- 1 medium onion (peeled & diced)
- 1 tbsp. of olive oil
- 2 cups of low-sodium chicken broth
- 2 sprigs of oregano
- 2 sprigs of thyme

Preparation:
1.    Pour the olive oil into the Instant Pot® and press Sauté to heat it. Include the mushrooms and onion, and cook for about 10 minutes, until the veggies are tender. Add the beef and cook for about 5 minutes, crumbling properly, until they are not pink anymore. Add the tomatoes, fennel, garlic, oregano, and thyme. Stir properly, then press Cancel.

2.    Add the spaghetti, broth, and sauce, and stir properly. Close the lid, set the steam release to Sealing, press Manual, and set the time to 8 minutes.

3.    Do a quick release of the pressure till the float valve drops as soon as the timer beeps. Open the lid and stir properly. Serve hot, topped with cheese.

**Nutritional Information per Serving:**
Calories: 188, carbs: 8g, fat: 7g, fiber: 2g, Protein: 23g, sodium: 595mg

# Ground Pork and Eggplant Casserole

Preparation time: 20 minutes, Cooking time: 18 minutes, Serves: 8

Ingredients:
- ⅛ tsp. of dried thyme
- ½ cup of low-sodium chicken broth
- ½ tsp. of ground black pepper
- ½ tsp. of hot sauce
- 1 large egg (beaten)
- 1 large yellow onion (peeled & diced)
- 1 medium green bell pepper (seeded & diced)
- 1 stalk celery (diced)
- 1 tbsp. of freeze-dried parsley
- 1 tsp. of salt
- 2 lb. (907 g) of lean ground pork
- 2 medium eggplants (cut into ½-inch pieces)
- 2 tsps. of Worcestershire sauce
- 3 tbsps. of tomato paste
- 4 cloves of garlic (peeled & minced)

Preparation:

1.     Press Sauté on the Instant Pot® then add the pork, onion, bell pepper, and celery to the pot. Cook for around 8 minutes till the pork changes color and breaks apart.

2.     Drain and get rid of the fat extracted from pork. Add the tomato paste, eggplant, garlic, thyme, hot sauce, parsley, Worcestershire sauce, pepper, salt, and egg. Stir properly and press Cancel.

3.     Add the chicken broth and close the lid. Set the steam release to Sealing, select Manual, and adjust the time to 10 minutes. After the timer beeps in about 25 minutes, allow the natural release of the pressure. Open the lid. Serve hot.

**Nutritional Information per Serving:**
Calories: 292, carbs: 10g, fat: 18g, fiber: 4g, Protein: 22g, sodium: 392mg

# Mediterranean Pork with Olives

Preparation time: 10 minutes, Cooking time: 6-8 hours, Serves: 4

Ingredients:
- ½ tsp. of black pepper (freshly ground)
- 1 cup of low-sodium chicken broth
- 1 pint of cherry tomatoes
- 1 small onion (sliced)
- 1 tsp. of dried oregano
- 1 tsp. of dried parsley
- 1 tsp. of sea salt
- 2 cups of whole green olives (pitted)
- 2 garlic cloves (minced)
- 4 pork chops (thick-cut & bone-in)
- Juice of 1 lemon

Preparation:
1.    Get a slow cooker and put the onion in it then place the pork chops over the top.

2.    Inside a small bowl, whisk the chicken broth, oregano, lemon juice, garlic, parsley, salt, and pepper together. Pour in the sauce and top with the tomatoes and olives.

3.    Cover with the lid and cook on low heat for 6-8 hours.

**Nutritional Information per Serving:**
Calories: 339, carbs: 6g, fat: 14g, fiber: 4g, Protein: 42g, sodium: 708mg

## Moroccan Lamb Roast

Preparation time: 15 minutes, Cooking time: 6-8 hours, Serves: 6

Ingredients:
- ¼ cup of fresh mint (chopped)
- ¼ cup of low-sodium chicken broth or low-sodium beef broth
- ¼ cup of onion (sliced)
- ½ tsp. of black pepper (freshly ground)
- ½ tsp. of ground cinnamon
- ½ tsp. of ground cloves
- ½ tsp. of ground coriander
- ½ tsp. of ground nutmeg
- ½ tsp. of sea salt
- 1 (3-lb./1.4-kg) lamb roast
- 1 tsp. of dried cumin
- 1 tsp. of dried ginger
- 1 tsp. of garlic powder
- 1 tsp. of ground turmeric
- 1 tsp. of paprika
- 1 tsp. of red pepper flakes
- 4 oz. (113 g) carrots (chopped)

Preparation:

1. Get a slow cooker and pour in the broth.

2. Get a small bowl and stir in the ginger, turmeric, cumin, garlic powder, paprika, red pepper flakes, coriander, cinnamon, nutmeg, cloves, black pepper, and salt together. Then firmly rub the mixture of spices over the entire lamb roast. Place the lamb inside the slow cooker, along with the onion and carrots.

3. Use the mint as a topping.

4.    Close the lid and let it cook on low heat for about 6-8 hours.

**Nutritional Information per Serving:**
Calories: 601, carbs: 4g, fat: 39g, fiber: 1g, Protein: 56g, sodium: 398mg

## Flank Steak and Blue Cheese Wraps

Preparation time: 20 minutes, Cooking time: 0 minutes, Serves: 6

Ingredients:
- ¼ cup of blue cheese crumbles
- ¼ cup of cherry tomatoes (chopped)
- ¼ cup of low-salt olives (pitted & chopped)
- ¼ cup of red onion (thinly sliced)
- ¼ cup of roasted red bell peppers (drained & coarsely chopped)
- 1 cup of leftover flank steak (cut into 1" slices)
- 6 whole-wheat / spinach wraps
- freshly ground pepper (to taste)
- Sea salt (to taste)

Preparation:
1.    Mix the flank steak, tomatoes, onion, olives, blue cheese, and bell pepper inside a small bowl.

2.    Spread a half cup of the flank steak mixture on each wrap. Roll halfway, folding the end in, then finish rolling it just like a burrito.

3.    If desired, cut diagonally, season with salt and pepper to taste, then serve.

**Nutritional Information per Serving:**
Calories: 158, carbs: 2g, fat: 8g, fiber: 1g, Protein: 20g, sodium: 150mg

## Herb-Roasted Beef Tips with Onions

Preparation time: 5 minutes, Cooking time: 10 minutes, Serves: 4

Ingredients:
- ½ tsp. of black pepper
- 1 lb. (454 g) of rib-eye steak (cubed)
- 1 tbsp. of fresh oregano
- 1 tsp. of salt
- 1 yellow onion (thinly sliced)
- 2 garlic cloves (minced)
- 2 tbsps. of olive oil

Preparation:
1.     Let the air fryer preheat to 380ºF or 193ºC.

2.     Mix the steak, oregano, garlic, onion, olive oil, salt, and pepper inside a medium bowl until the onion and beef are completely coated.

3.     Place the steak mixture in the air fryer basket and roast for about 5 minutes. Stir it and roast for an additional 5 minutes.

4.     Allow it to rest for about 5 minutes then serve alongside your favorite sides.

**Nutritional Information per Serving:**
Calories: 380, carbs: 3g, fat: 28g, fiber: 0g, Protein: 28g, sodium: 646mg

## *Garlic Balsamic London Broil*

Preparation time: 30 minutes, Cooking time: 8-10 minutes, Serves: 8

Ingredients:
- ½ tsp. of dried hot red pepper flakes
- 2 lb. (907 g) of London broil
- 2 tbsps. of olive oil
- 3 large minced garlic cloves
- 3 tbsps. o balsamic vinegar
- 3 tbsps. of whole-grain mustard
- Ground black pepper (to taste)
- Sea salt (to taste)

Preparation:
1.    Clean the London broil and score both sides.

2.    Mix the remaining ingredients thoroughly; then massage the mixture into all sides of the meat to coat. Allow it to marinate for a minimum of 3 hours.

3.    Set the air fryer to 204ºC (400ºF); cook the London broil for around 15 minutes. Flip it over then cook for an additional 10-12 minutes.

**Nutritional Information per Serving:**
Calories: 240, carbs: 2g, fat: 15g, fiber: 0g, Protein: 23g, sodium: 141mg

# Mediterranean Beef Steaks

Preparation time: 20 minutes, Cooking time: 20 minutes, Serves: 4

Ingredients:
- ½ tsp. of dried basil
- ½ tsp. of dried rosemary
- 1 tsp. of black pepper (freshly ground)
- 1 tsp. of sea salt (or more to taste)
- 2 tbsp. of olive oil
- 2 tbsps. of coconut aminos
- 2 tsps. of cayenne pepper (smoked)
- 3 heaping tbsps. of fresh chives
- 3 tbsps. of dry white wine
- 4 beef steaks (small-sized)

Preparation:

1.     Start by coating the steaks with basil, cayenne pepper, rosemary, black pepper, and salt.

2.     Drizzle olive oil, coconut aminos, and white wine over the steaks.

3.     Lastly, roast the steaks for 20 minutes in the air fryer set at 340°F or 171°C.

4.     Garnish with the fresh chives and serve.

## Nutritional Information per Serving:
Calories: 320, carbs: 5g, fat: 17g, fiber: 1g, Protein: 37g, sodium: 401mg

# CHAPTER FIVE

# BREAKFASTS

### *Avocado Toast with Smoked Trout*

Preparation time: 10 minutes, Cooking time: 0 minutes, Serves: 2

Ingredients:
- ¼ tsp. of kosher salt
- ¼ tsp. of lemon zest
- ¼ tsp. of red pepper flakes (add extra for sprinkling)
- ¾ tsp. of ground cumin
- 1 (3.75-oz. / 106-g) can of smoked trout
- 1 avocado (peeled & pitted)
- 2 pieces of toasted whole-wheat bread
- 2 tsps. of lemon juice (add extra for serving)

Preparation:
1.    Mash the lemon juice, avocado, cumin, lemon zest, salt, and red pepper flakes together inside a medium-sized bowl.

2.    Spread ½ of the mixture on each toasted bread piece. Use ½ of the smoked trout to top each of the toasted bread pieces.

3.    Garnish with a sprinkle of lemon juice (optional) and/or a pinch of red pepper flakes (optional).

**Nutritional Information per Serving:**
Calories: 300, carbs: 21g, fat: 20g, fiber: 6g, Protein: 11g, sodium: 390mg

## *Almond Butter Banana Chocolate Smoothie*

Preparation time: 5 minutes, Cooking time: 0 minutes, Serves: 1

Ingredients:

- ¾ cup of almond milk
- ½ medium banana (preferably frozen)
- ¼ cup of frozen blueberries
- 1 tbsp. of almond butter
- 1 tbsp. of unsweetened cocoa powder
- 1 tbsp. of chia seeds

Preparation:

1.    Put all the ingredients inside a blender or Vitamix. Blend until well combined. Serve.

## **Nutritional Information per Serving:**

Calories: 300, carbs: 37g, fat: 16g, fiber: 10g, Protein: 8g, sodium: 125mg

## *Fig and Ricotta Toast with Walnuts and Honey*

Preparation time: 5 minutes, Cooking time: 0 minutes, Serves: 2

Ingredients:
- ¼ cup  of ricotta cheese
- 1 tsp. of honey
- 2 pieces of whole-wheat bread (toasted)
- 2 tbsps. of chopped walnuts
- 4 halved figs

Preparation:

1.   Spread 2 tbsps. of the ricotta cheese on each of the pieces of toast. Press 4 fig halves firmly on each piece to ensure the figs remain the ricotta.

2.   Sprinkle the top with 1 tbsp. of walnuts then drizzle ½ tsp. of honey on each piece of the toast. Serve.

**Nutritional Information per Serving:**
Calories: 215, carbs: 26g, fat: 10g, fiber: 3g, Protein: 7g, sodium: 125mg

## Berry Warming Smoothie

Preparation time: 5 minutes, Cooking time: 0 minutes, Serves: 1

Ingredients:
- ⅛ tsp. of ground cardamom
- ¼ tsp. of grated ginger
- ¼ tsp. of ground cinnamon
- ¼ tsp. of ground nutmeg
- ¼ tsp. of vanilla extract (optional)
- ½ cup of baby spinach
- ½ cup of chopped cucumber
- ½ cup of frozen mixed berries
- 2 tbsps. of unsweetened shredded coconut
- ⅔ cup of plain yogurt or plain kefir

Preparation:
1. Put all the ingredients inside a blender or Vitamix. Blend until well combined. Serve.

**Nutritional Information per Serving:**
Calories: 165, carbs: 20g, fat: 7g, fiber: 4g, Protein: 7g, sodium: 100mg

## Mediterranean-Inspired White Smoothie

Preparation time: 5 minutes, Cooking time: 0 minutes, Serves: 1

Ingredients:
- ¼ cup of full-fat Greek yogurt
- ¼ tsp. of ground cinnamon
- ½ cup of low-fat 1% milk
- ½ medium apple (of any variety; peeled, halved, & seeded)
- ½ medium frozen banana (sliced; peel before freezing)
- ½ tsp. of honey
- 5 almonds (roasted)

Preparation:
1. Mix all the ingredients inside a blender. Blend until smooth.

2. Empty the blender into a glass and serve immediately. (This smoothie is best taken fresh.)

**Nutritional Information per Serving:**
Calories: 236, carbs: 40g, fat: 7g, fiber: 5g, Protein: 8g, sodium: 84mg

## Mediterranean Muesli and Breakfast Bowl

Prep time: 10 minutes | Cook time: 0 minutes | Serves 12

Ingredients:
Muesli:

- ½ cup of oat bran
- 1 cup of almonds or pistachios (coarsely chopped)
- 1 cup of rye flakes or wheat
- 3 cups of old-fashioned rolled oats
- 8 dates (chopped)
- 8 dried apricots (chopped
- 8 dried figs (chopped)
- Breakfast Bowl:
- ½ cup Mediterranean Muesli (above)
- ½ teaspoon black or white sesame seeds
- 1 cup low-fat plain Greek yogurt or milk
- 2 tablespoons pomegranate seeds (optional)

Preparation:
To prepare the muesli:
1.     Mix the wheat or rye flakes, oats, oat bran, pistachios or almonds, apricots, figs, and dates inside a medium bowl. Move them to an airtight bowl to store for as long as 1 month.
To prepare the breakfast bowl:
2.     Mix the muesli in a bowl with milk or yogurt. Top with the sesame seeds and the pomegranate seeds (optional).

**Nutritional Information per Serving:**
Calories: 234, carbs: 40g, fat: 6g, fiber: 6g, Protein: 8g, sodium: 54mg

## Smoked Salmon Egg Scramble with Dill and Chives

Preparation time: 5 minutes, Cooking time: 5 minutes, Serves: 2

Ingredients:
- ⅛ tsp. of black pepper (freshly ground)
- ¼ tsp. of kosher salt
- 1 tbsp. of fresh chives (minced)
- 1 tbsp. of fresh dill (minced)
- 1 tbsp. of milk
- 2 oz. (57 g) smoked salmon (thinly sliced)
- 2 tsp. of extra-virgin olive oil
- 4 large eggs

Preparation:

1.    Whisk the eggs, chives, milk, dill, pepper, and salt together inside a big bowl.

2.    Sauté the pan on medium heat or heat the olive oil inside a medium-sized skillet. Add the egg mixture and, stirring occasionally, cook for around 3 minutes.

3.    Add salmon and cook for around 1 minute till the eggs are set but still moist.

**Nutritional Information per Serving:**
Calories: 325, carbs: 1g, fat: 26g, fiber: 0g, Protein: 23g, sodium: 455mg

## Black Olive Toast with Herbed Hummus

Preparation time: 5 minutes, Cooking time: 5 minutes, Serves: 2

Ingredients:
- ¼ cup of store-bought plain hummus
- 1 clove of garlic (halved)
- 1 tbsp. of extra-virgin olive oil
- 1 tbsp. of fresh dill (finely chopped)
- 1 tbsp. of fresh mint (finely chopped)
- 1 tsp. of lemon peel (finely grated)
- 2 slices (½-inch thick) black olive bread
- 2 tbsps. of fresh flat-leaf parsley (finely chopped)

Preparation:

1.   Mix the hummus, lemon peel, and herbs inside a small-sized bowl.

2.   Toast the olive bread then rub it with the garlic immediately.

3.   Spread ½ of the hummus on each slice of bread then drizzle oil over it.

**Nutritional Information per Serving:**
Calories: 197, carbs: 20g, fat: 11g, fiber: 4g, Protein: 6g, sodium: 177mg

## *Breakfast Quinoa with Figs & Walnuts*

Preparation time: 10 minutes, Cooking time: 12 minutes, Serves: 4

Ingredients:
- ¼ tsp. of salt
- ½ cup of plain Greek yogurt (low-fat)
- ½ tsp. of ground cinnamon
- 1 cup of almond milk
- 1 cup of toasted walnuts (chopped)
- 1 tsp. of vanilla extract
- 1½ cups of quinoa (rinsed & drained)
- 2 tbsps. of honey
- 2½ cups of water
- 8 fresh figs (quartered)

Preparation:
1. Place the quinoa, almond milk, water, honey, cinnamon, vanilla, and salt inside the Instant Pot®. Stir well to mix. Close the lid and set the steam release to Sealing. Select Rice and set the timer to 12 minutes. After the timer beeps in about 20 minutes and naturally releases the pressure.

2. Select Cancel and open the lid. Use a fork to fluff the quinoa. Serve warm alongside yogurt, walnuts, and figs.

**Nutritional Information per Serving:**
Calories: 413, carbs: 52g, fat: 25g, fiber: 7g, Protein: 10g, sodium: 275mg

## *Savory Cottage Cheese Breakfast Bowl*

Preparation time: 10 minutes, Cooking time: 0 minutes, Serves: 4

Ingredients:
- ¼ cup of pitted kalamata olives (halved)
- ½ tsp. of ground black pepper
- 1 large tomato (chopped)
- 1 small cucumber (peeled & chopped)
- 1 tbsp. of extra-virgin olive oil
- 2 cups of low-fat cottage cheese
- 2 tbsps. of chopped mixed fresh herbs (e.g. basil, flat-leaf parsley, dill, and oregano)

Preparation:
1.    Mix the cottage cheese, pepper, and herbs inside a medium bowl. Then add the tomato, olives, and cucumber. Stir gently to combine then drizzle oil over it before serving.

**Nutritional Information per Serving:**
Calories: 181, carbs: 8g, fat: 10g, fiber: 1g, Protein: 15g, sodium: 788mg

# CHAPTER SIX

# DESSERTS

### *Ricotta Cheesecake*

Preparation time: 2 minutes, Cooking time: 45- 50 minutes, Serves: 12

Ingredients:
- 1 tsp. of vanilla extract
- 1¼ cups of sugar
- 2 cups of skim or fat-free ricotta cheese (one 15-oz. / 425-g container)
- 6 eggs
- Zest of 1 orange

Preparations:

1.    Let the oven preheat to 375ºF or 190ºC. Use cooking spray or butter to grease an 8" square baking pan.

2.    Stir the sugar and ricotta together inside a medium bowl. Add one egg at a time until all 6 eggs are well incorporated. Stir in the orange zest and vanilla.

3.    Transfer the batter to the already-prepared pan. Bake for 45-50 minutes or until set. Allow it to cool for 20 minutes inside the pan. Serve warm.

**Nutritional Information per Serving:**
Calories: 160, carbs: 15g, fat: 5g, fiber: 0g, Protein: 12g, sodium: 388mg

## Figs with Mascarpone and Honey

Preparation time: 5 minutes, Cooking time: 5 minutes, Serves: 4

Ingredients:
- ¼ cup of mascarpone cheese
- ¼ tsp. of flaked sea salt
- 1 tbsp. of honey
- 1/3 cup of walnuts (chopped)
- 8 fresh figs (halved)

Preparation:
1.    Toast the walnuts in a skillet placed over medium heat for about 3-5 minutes, stirring often.

2.    Arrange the figs on a platter or plate with the cut-side up. Then use your finger to create a small depression inside each fig's cut side and fill it with the mascarpone cheese.

3.    Sprinkle a bit of the walnut on top and drizzle with honey, then add a little pinch of the sea salt.

**Nutritional Information per Serving:**
Calories: 200, carbs: 24g, fat: 13g, fiber: 3g, Protein: 3g, sodium: 105mg

## Honey Ricotta with Espresso and Chocolate Chips

Preparation time: 5 minutes, Cooking time: 0 minutes, Serves: 2

Ingredients:
- 1 tsp. of chocolate shavings or dark chocolate chips
- 2 tbsps. of espresso (chilled or at room temperature)
- 2 tbsps. of honey
- 8 oz. (227 g) of ricotta cheese

Preparation:
1.    Whip the ricotta cheese and honey together inside a medium bowl for about 4 to 5 minutes until it turns smooth and light.

2.    Evenly spoon the mixture into two dessert bowls. Then drizzle 1 tbsp. of espresso into each of the dishes and sprinkle with chocolate shavings or chips.

**Nutritional Information per Serving:**
Calories: 235, carbs: 25g, fat: 10g, fiber: 0g, Protein: 13g, sodium: 115mg

## Strawberry-Pomegranate Molasses Sauce

Preparation time: 10 minutes, Cooking time: 5 minutes, Serves: 6

Ingredients:
- ¼ cup of honey
- 1-2 tbsps. of pomegranate molasses
- 2 pints of strawberries (hulled & halved)
- 2 tbsps. of chopped fresh mint
- 3 tbsps. of olive oil
- Greek yogurt - for serving

Preparation:
1. Pour the olive oil into a medium saucepan to heat over medium heat.

2. Add the hulled & halved strawberries and cook until the juices come out. Add the honey and stir then allow to cook for 1-2 minutes. Stir in the mint and molasses.

3. Serve warm on the Greek yogurt.

**Nutritional Information per Serving:**
Calories: 189, carbs: 24g, fat: 7g, fiber: 3g, Protein: 4g, sodium: 12mg

## Greek Yogurt Ricotta Mousse

Preparation time: 1 hr. 5 minutes, Cooking time: 0 minutes, Serves: 4

Ingredients:
- ½ tsp. of pure vanilla extract
- 2 tbsps. of granulated sugar
- 3 tsps. of fresh lemon juice
- 4½ oz. (128 g) 2% Greek yogurt
- 9 oz. (255 g) of full-fat ricotta cheese

Preparation:
1.    Mix all the ingredients inside a food processor. Blend for about 1 minute until smooth.

2.    Split the mousse among 4 serving glasses. Cover the glasses and refrigerate to cool for an hour before serving.

3.    Cover in the fridge and store for at least 4 days.

**Nutritional Information per Serving:**
Calories: 156, carbs: 10g, fat: 8g, fiber: 0g, Protein: 10g, sodium: 65mg

## Ricotta with Balsamic Cherries & Black Pepper

Preparation time: 10 minutes, Cooking time: 0 minutes, Serves: 4

Ingredients:
- 1 cup (8 oz. / 227 g) of ricotta
- 1 tsp. of vanilla extract
- 1½ tsps. of aged balsamic vinegar
- 2 tbsps. of honey
- 3 cups of halved pitted sweet cherries (if frozen, thaw)
- Pinch of black pepper (freshly ground)

Preparation:

1.    Mix the ricotta, vanilla, and honey in a food processor and blend until smooth. Pour the mixture into a medium bowl, then cover and refrigerate for an hour.

2.    Mix the vinegar, cherries, and pepper inside a small-sized bowl and stir until well mixed. Keep cooling alongside the ricotta mixture.

3.    To serve, spoon out the ricotta mixture into 4 serving glasses or bowls. Top each glass or bowl with equally divided cherries, then spoon a little accumulated juice on top.

4.    Serve chilled.

**Nutritional Information per Serving:**
Calories: 236, carbs: 42g, fat: 5g, fiber: 1g, Protein: 7g, sodium: 93mg

### *Whipped Greek Yogurt with Chocolate*

Preparation time: 10 minutes, Cooking time: 0 minutes, Serves: 4

Ingredients:
- 4 cups of plain full-fat Greek yogurt
- ½ cup of heavy (whipping) cream
- 2 oz. (57 g) of dark chocolate (at least 70% cacao; grated) for topping

Preparation:

1.    Whip the cream and yogurt for about 5 minutes inside the bowl of a stand mixer with a built-in whisk attachment or use a handheld mixer in a large bowl until peaks form.

2.    Share the whipped yogurt mixture evenly among 4 bowls and use the grated chocolate as a topping. Serve.

**Nutritional Information per Serving:**
Calories: 337, carbs: 19g, fat: 25g, fiber: 2g, Protein: 10g, sodium: 127mg

## *Greek Yogurt with Honey and Pomegranates*

Preparation time: 5 minutes, Cooking time: 0 minutes, Serves: 4

Ingredients:
- ¼ cup of honey
- ½ cup of pomegranate seeds
- 4 cups of plain full-fat Greek yogurt
- For the topping: Sugar (optional)

Preparation:

1.    Split the yogurt equally among 4 bowls. Split the pomegranate seeds equally among the bowls and drizzle honey over each of them.

2.    Sprinkle a pinch of sugar over each bowl, if desired, then serve.

**Nutritional Information per Serving:**
Calories: 232, carbs: 33g, fat: 8g, fiber: 1g, Protein: 9g, sodium: 114mg

## Slow-Cooked Fruit Medley

Preparation time: 10 minutes, Cooking time: 3-5 hours, Serves: 4-6

Ingredients:
- ⅓ cup of almond milk (or any low-sugar fruit juice you prefer)
- ½ cup of honey
- 1 lb. (454 g) of your preferred fresh or frozen fruit (stemmed & chopped as needed)
- Nonstick cooking spray

Preparation:

1.    Coat a slow cooker generously with cooking spray. Alternatively, you can use aluminum foil or parchment paper to line the cooker's bottom and sides.

2.    Add the milk and fruit to a slow cooker and stir gently to mix.

3.    Drizzle the honey over the fruit.

4.    Cover the slow cooker and cook on low heat for 3-5 hours.

**Nutritional Information per Serving:**
Calories: 192, carbs: 50g, fat: 0g, fiber: 3g, Protein: 1g, sodium: 27mg

## *Pears with Blue Cheese and Walnuts*

Preparation time: 10 minutes, Cooking time: 0 minutes, Serves: 1

Ingredients:
- ¼ cup of blue cheese crumbles
- 1 tbsp. of honey
- 1-2 pears (cored & sliced into 12 slices)
- 12 walnut halves

Preparation:

1.     Arrange the slices of pear on a plate, and use the blue cheese crumbles as a topping.

2.     Place 1 walnut on each slice and drizzle honey on top.

3.     Serve.

**Nutritional Information per Serving:**
Calories: 420, carbs: 35g, fat: 29g, fiber: 6g, Protein: 12g, sodium: 389mg

# CHAPTER SEVEN

# FISH & SEAFOOD

## *Flounder with Tomatoes and Basil*

Preparation time: 10 minutes, Cooking time: 20 minutes, Serves: 4

Ingredients:
- ¼ tsp. of black pepper (freshly ground)
- ½ tsp. of kosher salt
- 1 lb. (454 g) of cherry tomatoes
- 2 tbsps. of basil (cut into ribbons)
- 2 tbsps. of extra-virgin olive oil
- 2 tbsps. of lemon juice
- 4 (5- to 6-oz. / 142- to 170-g) of flounder fillets
- 4 garlic cloves (sliced)

Preparation:
1. Get the oven preheated to 425ºF or 220ºC.

2. Mix the tomatoes, olive oil, garlic, lemon juice, salt, basil, and black pepper very well inside a baking dish. Bake for around 5 minutes.

3. Get the baking dish out of the oven and lay the flounder on the tomato mixture. Let it bake for about 10 to 15 minutes until the fish turns opaque and starts to flake, depending on the thickness.

**Nutritional Information per Serving:**
Calories: 215, carbs: 6g, fat: 9g, fiber: 2g, Protein: 28g, sodium: 261mg

## Citrus–Marinated Scallops

Preparation time: 10 minutes, Cooking time: 10 minutes, Serves: 4

Ingredients:
- ¼ cup of extra-virgin olive oil
- 1 clove of garlic (minced)
- 1½ lb. (680 g) of dry scallops (with the side muscle removed)
- 2 lemons (Juice & zest)
- Freshly ground black pepper (to taste)
- Unrefined sea salt or salt (to taste)

Preparation:
1. Mix the lemon juice and zest, garlic, olive oil, pepper, and salt very well inside a big shallow bowl or baking dish. Add the scallops, cover, and place in the fridge for 1 hour.

2. Heat a big skillet on medium-high heat. Drain the scallops then place them inside a skillet. Allow each side to cook through for 4 to 5 minutes each.

## Nutritional Information per Serving:
Calories: 243, carbs: 7g, fat: 14g, fiber: 0g, Protein: 21g, sodium: 567mg

## Italian Halibut with Grapes and Olive Oil

Preparation time: 15 minutes, Cooking time: 20 minutes, Serves: 4

Ingredients:
- ¼ cup of extra-virgin olive oil
- ½ tsp. of unrefined sea salt or salt
- 1 small red chile pepper (finely chopped)
- 2 cups of seedless green grapes
- 4 boneless halibut fillets (4 oz. (113 g) each)
- 4 cloves of garlic (roughly chopped)
- A handful of fresh basil leaves (roughly torn)
- Black pepper (freshly ground)

Preparation:

1.    Inside a big, heavy-bottomed skillet placed over medium-high heat, pour in the olive oil and let it heat. Add the halibut, garlic, chile pepper, basil, grapes, salt, and pepper. Add 1¾ cups (410 ml) of water to the skillet then reduce the heat to medium-low. Cover and cook each side for 7 minutes until the fish turns opaque.

2.    Take the fish out of the pan and place it on a big serving dish. Increase the heat and cook for 30 seconds until the flavors in the sauce concentrate a little. Taste and adjust the seasoning.

3.    Pour the sauce on the fish and serve.

**Nutritional Information per Serving:**
Calories: 389, carbs: 15g, fat: 29g, fiber: 1g, Protein: 17g, sodium: 384mg

# Mussels with Tomatoes and Herbs

Preparation time: 15 minutes, Cooking time: 7 minutes, Serves: 6

Ingredients:
- ½ cup of vegetable broth
- ½ tsp. of ground black pepper
- ½ tsp. of ground fennel
- 1 (14½-oz. / 411-g) can of diced tomatoes (drained)
- 1 medium white onion (peeled & chopped)
- 2 cloves of garlic (peeled & minced)
- 2 tbsps. of chopped fresh dill
- 2 tbsps. of chopped fresh tarragon
- 2 tbsps. of light olive oil
- 3 lb. (1.4 kg) of mussels (scrubbed & beards removed)

Preparation:
1.    Select Sauté on the Instant Pot® and pour in the oil to heat. Add the onion and cook for about 3 minutes until tender. Add the garlic, tarragon, dill, pepper, and fennel, and cook for about 30 seconds until the garlic is fragrant. Select Cancel.

2.    Add the mussels, tomatoes, and broth. Stir to mix then close the lid, set the steam release to Sealing, select Manual, and set the time to three minutes. Quick-release the pressure as soon as the timer beeps until the float valve drops. Open the lid and get rid of any mussels that have not opened.

3.    Serve immediately.

**Nutritional Information per Serving:**
Calories: 162, carbs: 10g, fat: 7g, fiber: 2g, Protein: 14g, sodium: 435mg

## *Almond-Encrusted Salmon*

Preparation time: 10 minutes, Cooking time: 12 minutes, Serves: 4

Ingredients:
- ¼ cup of breadcrumbs
- ¼ cup of olive oil
- ½ cup of finely chopped almonds (lightly toasted)
- ½ tsp. of dried thyme
- 1 tbsp. of honey
- 4 salmon steaks
- Freshly ground pepper (to taste)
- Sea salt (to taste)

Preparation:

1.    Let the oven preheat to 350ºF or 180ºC.

2.    If necessary, place the honey inside the microwave for about 15 seconds to soften it for easier blending. Then mix the honey with the olive oil.

3.    Mix the breadcrumbs, thyme, almonds, freshly ground pepper, and sea salt inside a shallow dish.

4.    Use the olive oil mixture to coat the salmon steaks, before coating them with the almond mixture.

5.    Brush a baking sheet with olive oil and place the steaks on it to bake for 8 to 12 minutes, or until the salmon becomes firm and the almonds are browned lightly.

**Nutritional Information per Serving:**
Calories: 634, carbs: 12g, fat: 34g, fiber: 2g, Protein: 69g, sodium: 289mg

# Baked Grouper with Tomatoes & Garlic

Preparation time: 5 minutes, Cooking time: 12 minutes, Serves: 4

Ingredients:
- ¼ cup of fresh dill (roughly chopped)
- ¼ cup of Kalamata olives (sliced)
- ¼ cup of olive oil
- ½ tsp. of salt
- 1 tomato (sliced)
- 3 garlic cloves (minced)
- 4 grouper fillets
- Juice of 1 lemon

Preparation:

1.    Let the air fryer preheat to 380ºF or 193ºC.

2.    Season all sides of the grouper fillets with salt before placing them in the air fryer basket. Top with the tomato slices, minced garlic, olives, and fresh dill.

3.    Drizzle the olive oil and lemon juice on the grouper and bake for 10-12 minutes, or till the internal temperature gets to 145ºF or 63ºC.

**Nutritional Information per Serving:**
Calories: 379, carbs: 3g, fat: 17g, fiber: 1g, Protein: 51g, sodium: 492mg

## *Shrimp with Marinara Sauce*

Preparation time: 15 minutes, Cooking time: 6-7 hours, Serves: 4

Ingredients:
- ¼ tsp. of black pepper
- ½ tsp. of dried basil
- 1 (15-oz. / 425-g) can of diced tomatoes (with the juice)
- 1 (6-oz. / 170-g) can of tomato paste
- 1 clove of garlic (minced)
- 1 lb. (454 g) of cooked shrimp (peeled & deveined)
- 1 tsp. of dried oregano
- 1 tsp. of garlic powder
- 1½ tsps. of sea salt
- 2 tbsps. of fresh flat-leaf parsley (minced)
- ½ cup of grated parmesan cheese, for serving
- 2 cups of hot cooked spaghetti or linguine, for serving

Preparation:
1.    Mix the tomatoes, minced garlic, and tomato paste inside the slow cooker. Sprinkle the parsley, garlic powder, basil, oregano, pepper, and salt on it.

2.    Cover the cooker and cook for 6-7 hours on low heat.

3.    Increase to high heat, then add the cooked shrimp and stir. Cover and cook for about 15 minutes more on high.

4.    Serve hot on the cooked pasta and top with the Parmesan cheese.

**Nutritional Information per Serving:**
Calories: 313, carbs: 32g, fat: 5g, fiber: 7g, Protein: 39g, sodium: 876mg

# *Sea Bass with Roasted Root Vegetables*

Preparation time: 10 minutes, Cooking time: 15 minutes, Serves: 4

Ingredients:
- ¼ cup of olive oil
- ½ tsp. of onion powder
- 1 carrot (diced small)
- 1 lemon (sliced, with extra wedges for serving)
- 1 parsnip (diced small)
- 1 rutabaga (diced small)
- 1 tsp. of salt (divided)
- 2 garlic cloves (minced)
- 4 sea bass fillets

Preparation:
1. Let the air fryer preheat to 380ºF or 193ºC.

2. Toss the carrot, rutabaga, and parsnip in a small bowl with 1 tsp. of salt and olive oil.

3. Season the sea bass lightly with the leftover 1 tsp. of salt and onion powder. Place it in a single layer inside the air fryer basket.

4. Spread the garlic on the top of each fillet, then top with the lemon slices.

5. Place the prepared vegetables around and on the fish, all inside the basket. Roast for about 15 minutes.

6. Serve with extra lemon wedges, as preferred.

**Nutritional Information per Serving:**
Calories: 295, carbs: 12g, fat: 16g, fiber: 3g, Protein: 25g, sodium: 687mg

## Whitefish with Lemon and Capers

Preparation time: 5 minutes, Cooking time: 20 minutes, Serves: 4

Ingredients:
- ½ tsp. of black pepper (freshly ground)
- 1 tbsp. of extra-virgin olive oil
- 1 tsp. of salt (divided)
- 2 tbsps. of capers (drained)
- 3 tbsps. of lemon juice
- 4 (4- to 5-oz. / 113- to 142-g) of cod fillets (or any other whitefish)
- 4 tbsps. (½ stick) of unsalted butter

Preparation:

1.    Let the oven preheat to 450ºF or 235ºC. Place the cod inside a big baking dish. Drizzle with ½ teaspoon of salt and olive oil, then bake for about 15 minutes.

2.    Just before the fish finishes cooking, place the butter inside a small saucepan to melt over medium heat. Then add the capers, leftover ½ tsp. of salt, lemon juice, and pepper; let it simmer for about 30 seconds.

3.    Lay the fish inside a serving dish after baking; then spoon out the caper sauce and place it over the fish.

4.    Serve.

**Nutritional Information per Serving:**
Calories: 255, carbs: 1g, fat: 16g, fiber: 0g, Protein: 26g, sodium: 801mg

# *Parmesan Mackerel with Coriander*

Preparation time: 10 minutes, Cooking time: 7 minutes, Serves: 2

Ingredients:
- 1 tbsp. of olive oil
- 1 tsp. of ground coriander
- 2 oz. of (57 g) Parmesan (grated)
- 12 oz. (340 g) mackerel fillet

Preparation:

1. Sprinkle olive oil over the mackerel fillet and place it inside the air fryer basket.

2. Top with the grated Parmesan and ground coriander.

3. Cook the fish for 7 minutes at 390°F or 199°C.

**Nutritional Information per Serving:**
Calories: 522, carbs: 1g, fat: 39g, fiber: 0g, Protein: 42g, sodium: 544mg

# CHAPTER EIGHT

# PASTA

### *Avgolemono*

Preparation time: 10 minutes, Cooking time: 3 minutes, Serves: 6

Ingredients:
- ¼ cup of lemon juice
- ½ cup of orzo
- ½ tsp. of ground black pepper
- ½ tsp. of salt
- 1 tbsp. of fresh flat-leaf parsley (chopped)
- 1 tbsp. of olive oil
- 12 oz. (340 g) of cooked chicken breast (shredded)
- 2 large eggs
- 2 tbsps. of fresh dill (chopped)
- 6 cups of chicken stock

Preparation:

1.      Put the stock, olive oil, and orzo into the Instant Pot®. Then close the lid, set the steam release to Sealing, select Manual, and adjust the time to three minutes. As soon as the timer beeps, quick release of the pressure till the float valve drops. Then open the lid and add the chicken, pepper, and salt then stir.

2.      Mix the eggs and lemon juice inside a medium bowl then whisk slowly in the hot cooking liquid gotten from the Instant pot, a quarter cup at a time, till you've added 1 cup of liquid. Add egg mixture to the soup immediately and stir very well. Allow it to stand on Keep Warm setting for 10 minutes, stirring occasionally.

3.      Add the parsley and dill. Then serve immediately.

**Nutritional Information per Serving:**
Calories: 193, carbs: 15g, fat: 5g, fiber: 1g, Protein: 21g, sodium: 552mg

# *Tahini Soup*

Preparation time: 5 minutes, Cooking time: 4 minutes, Serves: 6

Ingredients:
- ¼ cup of lemon juice
- ½ cup of tahini
- ½ tsp. of ground black pepper
- 1 tbsp. of olive oil
- 1 tsp. of salt
- 2 cups of orzo
- 8 cups of water

Preparation:
1.     Put the pasta, oil, water, pepper, and salt into the Instant Pot®. Then close the lid, set steam release to Sealing, select Manual, and set the time to 4 minutes. As soon as the timer beeps, do a quick release of the pressure, and when the float valve drops, open the lid. Set it aside.

2.     Add the tahini to a small mixing bowl then add the lemon juice slowly while whisking continuously. When the lemon juice is well incorporated, take around ½ cup of hot broth out of the pot and add to the tahini mixture slowly while whisking till it turns creamy and smooth.

3.     Pour the mixture into the soup, mix very well, and serve immediately.

**Nutritional Information per Serving:**
Calories: 338, carbs: 49g, fat: 13g, fiber: 5g, Protein: 12g, sodium: 389mg

## Pasta Salad with Tomato, Arugula, & Feta

Preparation time: 10 minutes, Cooking time: 4 minutes, Serves: 8

Ingredients:
- ½ tsp. of ground black pepper
- ½ tsp. of salt
- 1 cup of crumbled feta cheese
- 1 lb. (454 g) of rotini
- 1 medium-sized red bell pepper (seeded & diced)
- 2 cloves of garlic (peeled & minced)
- 2 medium Roma tomatoes (diced)
- 2 tbsps. of white wine vinegar
- 3 tbsps. of extra-virgin olive oil (divided)
- 4 cups of water
- 5 oz. (142 g) of baby arugula

Preparation:

1.    Add pasta, 1 tbsp. of oil, and water to the Instant Pot®. Close the lid, set the steam release to Sealing, select Manual, and set the time to 4 minutes. As soon as the timer beeps, do a quick release of the pressure till the float valve drops. Open the lid, drain the pasta, then rinse it with cold water and set it aside.

2.    Mix the remaining 2 tbsps. of oil, garlic, tomatoes, bell pepper, cheese, arugula, and vinegar inside a big bowl. Stir in the pasta and use pepper and salt to season it. Cover with the lid and place in the fridge for 2 hours before serving.

**Nutritional Information per Serving:**
Calories: 332, carbs: 44g, fat: 12g, fiber: 3g, Protein: 12g, sodium: 480mg

## Bowtie Pesto Pasta Salad

Preparation time: 5 minutes, Cooking time: 4 minutes, Serves: 8

Ingredients:
- ½ cup of fresh basil (chopped)
- ½ cup of grated Parmesan cheese
- ½ cup of prepared pesto
- ½ tsp. of ground black pepper
- 1 lb. (454 g) of whole-wheat bowtie pasta
- 1 tbsp. of extra-virgin olive oil
- 2 cups of baby spinach
- 2 cups of cherry tomatoes (halved)
- 4 cups of water

Preparation:

1.	Put the pasta, olive oil, and water inside the Instant Pot®. Close the lid, set the steam release to Sealing, select Manual, and set the timer on 4 minutes.

2.	After the timer beeps, do a quick release of the pressure till the float valve drops then open the lid. Drain any excess liquid. Let the pasta cool to room temperature for around 30 minutes.

3.	Stir in the tomatoes, basil, spinach, pesto, cheese, and pepper. Place in the refrigerator for 2 hours. Stir properly and serve.

**Nutritional Information per Serving:**
Calories: 360, carbs: 44g, fat: 12g, fiber: 13g, Protein: 16g, sodium: 372mg

# Couscous with Crab & Lemon

Preparation time: 10 minutes, Cooking time: 7 minutes, Serves: 4

Ingredients:
- ¼ cup of fresh flat-leaf parsley (minced)
- ¼ cup of grated Parmesan cheese
- ½ tsp. of ground black pepper
- 1 clove of garlic (peeled & minced)
- 1 cup of couscous
- 1 tbsp. of fresh dill (minced)
- 2 cups of water
- 3 tbsps. of extra-virgin olive oil (divided)
- 3 tbsps. of lemon juice
- 8 oz. (227 g) jumbo lump crabmeat

Preparation:
1.    Place the couscous, 1 tbsp. of oil, water, and garlic into the Instant Pot®. Stir properly and close the lid. Set the steam release to Sealing, select Manual, and set the time to 7 minutes. After the timer beeps, allow the pressure to release naturally for ten minutes, then quick-release the leftover pressure and then open the lid.

2.    Use a fork to fluff the couscous. Add the parsley, crabmeat, dill, lemon juice, remaining 2 tablespoons oil, and pepper. Stir to mix. Use the cheese to top then serve immediately.

**Nutritional Information per Serving:**
Calories: 360, carbs: 34g, fat: 15g, fiber: 2g, Protein: 22g, sodium: 388mg

## Pasta with Marinated Artichokes and Spinach

Preparation time: 10 minutes, Cooking time: 5 minutes, Serves: 6

Ingredients:
- ¼ tsp. of salt
- ½ cup of grated Parmesan cheese
- 1 cup of drained & marinated artichoke hearts
- 1 lb. (454 g) of whole-wheat spaghetti (broken in half)
- 1 tsp. of ground black pepper
- 2 cups of baby spinach
- 2 tbsps. of fresh flat-leaf parsley (chopped)
- 2 tbsps. of fresh oregano (chopped)
- 3½ cups of water
- 4 tbsps. of extra-virgin olive oil (divided)

Preparation:

1.    Put the pasta, 2 tbsps. of oil, salt, and water into the Instant Pot®. Shut the lid, set the steam release to Sealing, select Manual, and set the time to 5 minutes.

2.    After the timer beeps, do a quick release of the pressure till the float valve drops, then open the lid. Drain the excess liquid then stir in the spinach and leftover 2 tbsps. of oil.

3.    Toss well until the spinach wilts. Stir in the oregano, artichokes, and parsley. When they're well mixed, sprinkle pepper and cheese over it and serve immediately.

**Nutritional Information per Serving:**
Calories: 414, carbs: 56g, fat: 16g, fiber: 9g, Protein: 16g, sodium: 467mg

## Spaghetti with Fresh Mint Pesto and Ricotta Salata

Preparation time: 5 minutes, Cooking time: 15 minutes, Serves: 4

Ingredients:
- ¼ cup of slivered almonds
- ¼ tsp. of black pepper (freshly ground)
- ⅓ cup of olive oil
- ½ cup of freshly grated ricotta Salata (add extra for garnish)
- 1 lb. (454 g) of spaghetti
- 1 tbsp. of lemon juice & ½ tsp. of lemon zest from 1 lemon
- 2 cups of packed fresh mint leaves (add extra for garnish)
- 3 medium garlic cloves

Preparation:

1. Pour salted water into a large pot set over high heat. Let it boil for the spaghetti.

2. Mix the almonds, lemon juice and zest, mint leaves, garlic, pepper, and olive oil inside a food processor and pulse until you get a smooth paste. Add the cheese to the processor and pulse until well combined.

3. When the water starts to boil, add the spaghetti and cook following the instructions on the pack. Drain the spaghetti and put it back into the pot.

4. Put the pesto inside the pasta and toss to properly coat the spaghetti. Garnish with extra cheese and mint leaves (optional). Serve hot.

**Nutritional Information per Serving:**
Calories: 619, carbs: 70g, fat: 31g, fiber: 4g, Protein: 21g, sodium: 113mg

## Penne with Tuna and Green Olives

Preparation time: 5 minutes, Cooking time: 5 minutes, Serves: 4

Ingredients:
- ¼ tsp. of black pepper (freshly ground)
- ½ cup of green olives
- ½ tsp. of salt
- ½ tsp. of wine vinegar
- 2 (6-oz. / 170-g) cans of tuna in olive oil (do not drain the oil)
- 2 tbsps. of flat-leaf parsley (chopped)
- 2 tbsps. of olive oil
- 3 garlic cloves (minced)
- 12 oz. (340 g) of penne pasta (cooked in line with package directions)

Preparation:

1.     Pour the olive oil into a medium skillet to heat over medium heat. Put the garlic in the oil and cook for 2 to 3 minutes, stirring continuously until the garlic starts to brown. Then add the olives, tuna with its oil, pepper, and salt. Stirring continuously, cook for 1 or two minutes until the ingredients are heated through. Take it off the heat then stir the vinegar in.

2.     Put the cooked pasta inside the skillet and toss gently to coat it well with the sauce. Garnish with the parsley and serve instantly.

**Nutritional Information per Serving:**
Calories: 511, carbs: 52g, fat: 22g, fiber: 1g, Protein: 31g, sodium: 826mg

## *Greek Chicken Pasta Casserole*

Preparation time: 15 minutes, Cooking time: 4-6 hours, Serves: 4

Ingredients:
- ¼ cup of crumbled feta cheese
- ¼ cup of whole Kalamata olives (pitted)
- ½ red onion (diced)
- ½ tsp. of black pepper (freshly ground)
- 1 tsp. of extra-virgin olive oil
- 1 tsp. of sea salt
- 2 lb. (907 g) of boneless, skinless chicken breasts or thighs (cut into 1" pieces)
- 2 tbsps. of red wine vinegar
- 2 tsps. of dried oregano
- 3 garlic cloves (minced)
- 3 Roma tomatoes (diced)
- 7 cups of low-sodium chicken broth
- 8 oz. (227 g) of dried rotini pasta

Preparation:
1.    Mix the chicken, chicken broth, pasta, onion, tomatoes, garlic, olives, oregano, vinegar, olive oil, pepper, and salt inside a slow cooker. Stir it to mix properly.

2.    Cover the cooker and cook on Low heat for 4-6 hours.

3.    To serve, garnish with feta cheese.

**Nutritional Information per Serving:**
Calories: 608, carbs: 55g, fat: 17g, fiber: 8g, Protein: 59g, sodium: 775mg

## Spicy Broccoli Pasta Salad

Preparation time: 10 minutes, Cooking time: 10 minutes, Serves: 2

Ingredients:

- ¼ cup of plain Greek yogurt
- 1 cup of carrots (peeled & shredded)
- 1 tsp. of red pepper flakes
- 2 cups of broccoli florets
- 8 oz. (227 g) of whole-wheat pasta
- Freshly ground pepper (to taste)
- Juice of 1 lemon
- Sea salt (to taste)

Preparation:

1. Cook the pasta in line with the package instructions for al dente. Drain properly.

2. When the pasta cools down, mix it inside a big bowl with the vegetables, yogurt, red pepper flakes, and lemon juice, and stir very well to combine.

3. If necessary, adjust the seasoning, adding freshly ground pepper and sea salt as required.

4. Serve chilled or at room temperature.

**Nutritional Information per Serving:**
Calories: 473, carbs: 101g, fat: 2g, fiber: 13g, Protein: 22g, sodium: 101mg

# CHAPTER NINE

# PIZZAS, WRAPS, AND SANDWICHES

### *Turkey Burgers with Feta and Dill*

Preparation time: 5 minutes, Cooking time: 15 minutes, Serves: 4

Ingredients:
- 1 lb. (454 g) of ground turkey breast
- 1 small red onion (½ finely chopped & ½ sliced)
- ½ cup of crumbled feta cheese
- ¼ cup of chopped fresh dill
- 1 clove of garlic (minced)
- ½ tsp. of kosher salt
- ¼ tsp. of ground black pepper
- 4 whole grain hamburger rolls
- 4 thick slices of tomato
- 4 lettuce leaves

Preparation:
1.  Use olive oil to coat a grill pan or grill rack and set to medium-high heat.

2.  Using your hands, mix the turkey, cheese, chopped onion, dill, salt, garlic, and pepper inside a big bowl. Avoid over-mixing. Split into 4 patties, 4 inches in diameter.

3.  Cover the patties and grill each side for 5-6 minutes until a thermometer shows 165ºF (74ºC) when inserted in the center.

4.  To serve, lay each patty on a roll along with the 1 lettuce leaf, sliced onion, and 1 tomato slice.

**Nutritional Information per Serving:**
Calories: 305, carbs: 26g, fat: 7g, fiber: 3g, Protein: 35g, sodium: 708mg

# Chicken and Goat Cheese Pizza

Preparation time: 10 minutes, Cooking time: 10 minutes, Serves: 4

Ingredients:
- 1 cup of shredded cooked chicken
- 1 lb. (454 g) of premade pizza dough
- 2 tbsps. of olive oil
- 3 oz. (85 g) of goat cheese (crumbled)
- All-purpose flour (for dusting)
- Black pepper (freshly ground)
- Sea salt

Preparation:
1. Let the oven preheat to 475ºF or 245ºC.

2. Roll out the dough on a floured surface to a 12" round and lay it on a baking sheet or pizza pan that has been lightly floured. Drizzle olive oil on the dough and evenly spread it out. Top it with goat cheese and chicken.

3. Let the pizza bake for 8-10 minutes, till the crust is thoroughly cooked and golden.

4. Use pepper and salt to season then serve.

## Nutritional Information per Serving:
Calories: 555, carbs: 60g, fat: 23g, fiber: 2g, Protein: 24g, sodium: 660mg

# Grilled Chicken Salad Pita

Preparation time: 15 minutes, Cooking time: 16 minutes, Serves: 1

Ingredients:
- ½ small cucumber (chopped)
- ½ small red onion (thinly sliced)
- 1 boneless & skinless chicken breast
- 1 cup of baby spinach
- 1 roasted red pepper (sliced)
- 1 tbsp. of olive oil
- 1 tomato (chopped)
- 1 whole-wheat pita pocket
- 2 tbsps. of crumbled feta cheese
- freshly ground pepper (to taste)
- Juice of 1 lemon
- Sea salt (to taste)

Preparation:

1.    Preheat a charcoal or gas grill till it gets to medium-high heat.

2.    Use freshly ground pepper and sea salt to season the chicken breast then grill each side for around 7 to 8 minutes until they are cooked through.

3.    Let the chicken rest for about 5 minutes before you slice them into strips.

4.    As the chicken cooks, add all your chopped veggies to a medium-sized mixing bowl and use freshly ground pepper and sea salt to season.

5.    Cut the chicken into cubes then add them to the salad. Pour in the lemon juice and olive oil then toss properly.

6.    Stuff your mixture into a pita pocket, using the feta cheese as a topping. Serve instantly.

## Nutritional Information per Serving:
Calories: 653, carbs: 34g, fat: 26g, fiber: 6g, Protein: 71g, sodium: 464mg

### *Mediterranean Tuna Salad Sandwiches*
Preparation time: 10 minutes, Cooking time: 5 minutes, Serves: 2

Ingredients:
- ¼ cup of plain Greek yogurt
- ½ small red onion (diced)
- 1 can of white tuna, packed inside olive oil or water (drained)
- 1 roasted red pepper (diced)
- 1 tbsp. of flat-leaf parsley (chopped)
- 4 whole-grain pieces of bread (whole-grain)
- 10 low-salt olives (pitted & finely chopped)
- Freshly ground pepper (to taste)
- Juice of 1 lemon
- Sea salt (to taste)

Preparation:
1.    Mix all of the ingredients, excluding the bread, inside a small bowl. Mix thoroughly.

2.    Use freshly ground pepper and sea salt to season to taste. Then warm the bread in a pan or toast it.

3.    Prepare the sandwich then serve instantly.

**Nutritional Information per Serving:**

Calories: 307, carbs: 31g, fat: 7g, fiber: 5g, Protein: 30g, sodium: 564mg

## Greek Salad Pita

Preparation time: 15 minutes, Cooking time: 0 minutes, Serves: 4

Ingredients:
- ½ cup of baby spinach leaves
- ½ small cucumber (chopped & deseeded)
- ½ small red onion (thinly sliced)
- ½ tbsp. of red wine vinegar
- 1 cup of romaine lettuce (chopped)
- 1 tbsp. of crumbled feta cheese
- 1 tomato (chopped & seeded)
- 1 tsp. of Dijon mustard
- 1 whole-wheat pita
- 2 tbsps. of olive oil
- Freshly ground pepper (to taste)
- Sea salt (to taste)

Preparation:

1.     Mix everything excluding the freshly ground pepper, sea salt, and pita bread inside a medium bowl.

2.     Toss well to combine the salad.

3.     Use freshly ground pepper and sea salt to season to taste. Then stuff the salad mixture into the pita. Serve!

**Nutritional Information per Serving:**
Calories: 123, carbs: 12g, fat: 8g, fiber: 2g, Protein: 3g, sodium: 125mg

## Cucumber Basil Sandwiches

Preparation time: 10 minutes, Cooking time: 0 minutes, Serves: 2

Ingredients:
- ¼ cup of hummus
- 1 large cucumber (thinly sliced)
- 4 slices of whole-grain bread
- 4 whole basil leaves

Preparation:

1.    Spread hummus over 2 bread slices, and lay the cucumbers on it. Use the basil to top the sandwiches then close them.

2.    Press the sandwiches down lightly then serve instantly.

### Nutritional Information per Serving:
Calories: 209, carbs: 32g, fat: 5g, fiber: 6g, Protein: 9g, sodium: 275mg

## Mediterranean-Pita Wraps

Preparation time: 5 minutes, Cooking time: 14 minutes, Serves: 4

Ingredients:
- ½ tsp. of chili powder
- 1 lb. (454 g) of mackerel fish fillets
- 1 tbsp. of Mediterranean seasoning mix
- 2 oz. (57 g) of feta cheese (crumbled)
- 2 tbsps. of olive oil
- 4 tortillas
- Freshly ground black pepper (to taste)
- Sea salt (to taste)

Preparation:
1.    Toss the olive oil and the fish fillets, then lay them in a lightly oiled air fryer basket.

2.    Let the fish fillets air fry for approximately 14 minutes at 400ºF or 204ºC, flipping them over about halfway through cooking time.

3.    Arrange your pitas with the fish and leftover ingredients.

4.    Serve warm.

**Nutritional Information per Serving:**
Calories: 275, carbs: 13g, fat: 13g, fiber: 2g, Protein: 27g, sodium: 322mg

### *Pesto Chicken Mini Pizzas*

Preparation time: 5 minutes, Cooking time: 10 minutes, Serves: 4

Ingredients:
- ¾ cup of pesto
- 2 cups of cooked chicken (shredded)
- 2 cups of Mozzarella cheese (shredded)
- 4 English muffins  (split)

Preparation:
1.    Toss the chicken along with the pesto inside a medium-sized bowl. Lay 1/8 of the chicken over each half of the English muffin. Top every single English muffin with a quarter cup of Mozzarella cheese.

2.      Place the pizzas, 4 at a time, inside the air fryer. Air fry for 5 minutes at 350ºF or 177ºC. Repeat the same process with the remaining 4 pizzas.

## Nutritional Information per Serving:
Calories: 617, carbs: 29g, fat: 36g, fiber: 3g, Protein: 45g, sodium: 544mg

## Mexican Pizza

Preparation time: 10 minutes, Cooking time: 7-9 minutes, Serves: 4

Ingredients:
- ½ cup of salsa
- ½ cup of shredded Colby cheese
- ¹/₃ cup of sour cream
- ¾ cup of refried beans (from a 16-oz. / 454-g can)
- 1 cup of shredded pepper Jack cheese
- 1 jalapeño pepper (sliced)
- 4 whole-wheat pita bread
- 10 frozen precooked beef meatballs (thawed & sliced)

Preparation:
1.    Mix the refried beans, jalapeño pepper, meatballs, and salsa inside a medium-sized bowl.

2.    Let the air fryer preheat for 3-4 minutes or until it becomes hot.

3.    Top up the pitas with a mixture of refried beans and sprinkle the cheeses on top.

4.    Let it bake for 7-9 minutes at 370ºF or 188ºC or till the pizza becomes crisp while the cheese melts and starts browning.

5.    Top every single pizza with one dollop of sour cream. Serve warm.

**Nutritional Information per Serving:**
Calories: 484, carbs: 32g, fat: 30g, fiber: 7g, Protein: 24g, sodium: 612mg

## Dill Salmon Salad Wraps

Preparation time: 10 minutes, Cooking time: 10 minutes, Serves: 6

Ingredients:
- ¼ tsp. of sea salt or kosher
- ½ cup of diced carrots (approximately 1 carrot)
- ½ cup of diced celery (approximately 1 celery stalk)
- ½ tsp. of freshly ground black pepper
- 1 lb. (454 g) of salmon filet (cooked & flaked), or 3 (5-oz. / 142-g) cans of salmon
- 1 tbsp. of aged balsamic vinegar
- 1½ tbsps. of extra-virgin olive oil
- 2 tbsps. of capers
- 3 tbsps. of chopped fresh dill
- 3 tbsps. of diced red onion (a little smaller than ⅛ onion)
- 4 whole-wheat flatbread wraps or soft whole-wheat tortillas

Preparation:
1.    Mix the salmon, celery, carrots, dill, capers, red onion, oil, vinegar, salt, and pepper inside a large bowl.

2.    Split the salmon salad between the flatbreads. Then fold up the flatbread's bottom and roll the wrap-up. Serve.

Nutritional Information per Serving:
Calories: 185, carbs: 12g, fat: 8g, fiber: 2g, Protein: 17g, sodium: 237mg

# CHAPTER TEN

# POULTRY

## *Za'atar Chicken Tenders*

Prep time: 5 minutes | Cook time: 15 minutes | Serves 4

Ingredients:
- ¼ tsp. of freshly ground black pepper
- ½ tsp. of kosher salt
- 1 lb. (454 g) of chicken tenders
- 1½ tbsps. of za'atar
- Olive oil cooking spray

Preparation:

1.   Let the oven preheat to 450ºF or 235ºC. Then use foil or parchment paper to line a baking sheet and spray lightly with the olive oil cooking spray.

2.   Mix the chicken, black pepper, za'atar, and salt inside a big bowl. Mix properly, fully covering the chicken tenders. Lay on the baking sheet in a single layer and bake for around 15 minutes; halfway through the cooking time, flip the chicken over.

## Nutritional Information per Serving:
Calories: 145, carbs: 0g, fat: 4g, fiber: 0g, Protein: 26g, sodium: 190mg

## *Harissa Yogurt Chicken Thighs*

Preparation time: 5 minutes, Cooking time: 25 minutes-, Serves: 4

Ingredients:
- ¼ tsp. of black pepper (freshly ground)
- ½ cup of plain Greek yogurt
- ½ tsp. of kosher salt
- 1 tbsp. of lemon juice
- 1½ lb. (680 g) of boneless & skinless chicken thighs
- 2 tbsps. of harissa

Preparation:

1.    Mix the yogurt, lemon juice, harissa, black pepper, and salt inside a bowl. Include the chicken then combine well. Marinate for a minimum of 15 minutes, and as long as 4 hours inside the refrigerator.

2.    Let the oven preheat to 425ºF or 220ºC. Use foil or parchment paper to line a baking sheet. Take the chicken thighs out of the marinade then lay them out on the baking sheet in a single layer. Roast for about 20 minutes and halfway through the time, turn the chicken over.

3.    Change the temperature of the oven to broil. Then broil the chicken for 2-3 minutes until some spots turn golden brown.

**Nutritional Information per Serving:**
Calories: 190, carbs: 1g, fat: 10g, fiber: 0g, Protein: 24g, sodium: 230mg

# Turkey Breast in Yogurt Sauce

Preparation time: 10 minutes, Cooking time: 16 minutes, Serves: 6

Ingredients:
- ¼ tsp. of salt
- ½ tsp. of ground black pepper
- 1 (1 lb. / 454-g) bag of frozen baby peas & pearl onions (thawed)
- 1 cup of plain low-fat yogurt
- 1 lb. (454 g) of boneless turkey breast (cut into bite-sized pieces)
- 1 tbsp. of olive oil
- 1 tsp. of ground cumin
- 1 tsp. of ground turmeric
- 1 tsp. of yellow mustard seeds

Preparation:

1.    Mix the yogurt, cumin, turmeric, mustard seeds, pepper, and salt inside a big bowl. Then stir in the turkey. Cover it and place it in the fridge for 4 hours.

2.    Press Sauté on the Instant Pot® then heat the oil. Add the mixture of turkey and yogurt. Press Cancel, close the lid, set the steam release to Sealing, then press Manual, and set the time to eight minutes. After the timer beeps, do a quick release of the pressure then open the lid.

3.    Stir in the peas and onions. Then press Cancel, select Sauté, and simmer for about 8 minutes till the sauce thickens. Serve hot.

**Nutritional Information per Serving:**
Calories: 146, carbs: 7g, fat: 6g, fiber: 1g, Protein: 17g, sodium: 554mg

# Chicken with Dates and Almonds

Preparation time: 15 minutes, Cooking time: 6-8 hours, Serves 4

Ingredients:
- ¼ cup of sliced almonds
- ¼ tsp. of black pepper (freshly ground)
- ¼ tsp. of ground cinnamon
- ½ cup of dried dates
- ½ cup of low-sodium chicken broth
- ½ tsp. of ground coriander
- ½ tsp. of ground ginger
- 1 (15-oz. / 425-g) can of reduced-sodium chickpeas (drained & rinsed)
- 1 onion (sliced)
- 1 tsp. of ground cumin
- 1 tsp. of sea salt
- 2 garlic cloves (minced)
- 2½ lb. (1.1 kg) chicken thighs (bone-in, skin-on)

Preparation:
1.    Gently toss the chickpeas and onion together inside a slow cooker.

2.    Put the chicken on the chickpea mixture then pour the chicken broth on top of the chicken.

3.    Stir the garlic, cumin, salt, ginger, cinnamon, coriander, and pepper together inside a small bowl. Sprinkle everything with the spice mix.

4.    Top with almonds and dates.

5.    Cover the cooker then cook on low heat for 6-8 hours.

**Nutritional Information per Serving:**
Calories: 841, carbs: 41g, fat: 48g, fiber: 9g, Protein: 57g, sodium: 812mg

## Deconstructed Greek Chicken Kebabs

Preparation time: 20 minutes, Cooking time: 6-8 hours, Serves: 4

Ingredients:
- ¼ tsp. of black pepper (freshly ground)
- ½ tsp. of dried basil
- ½ tsp. of dried thyme
- 1 green bell pepper (seeded & cut into 1" pieces)
- 1 large red onion (chopped)
- 1 red bell pepper (seeded & cut into 1" pieces)
- 1 tbsp. of red wine vinegar
- 1 tsp. of dried oregano
- 1 tsp. of sea salt
- 2 garlic cloves (minced)
- 2 lb. (907 g) of boneless, skinless chicken thighs (cut into 1-inch cubes)
- 2 tbsps. of extra-virgin olive oil
- 2 tbsps. of lemon juice (freshly squeezed)
- 2 zucchini (almost 1 lb. / 454 g) (cut into 1" pieces)

Preparation:
1.    Mix the chicken, green & red bell peppers, zucchini, onion, lemon juice, olive oil, vinegar, salt, garlic, oregano, basil, black pepper, and thyme inside a slow cooker. Stir until well mixed.

2.    Close the cooker then cook on low heat for 6-8 hours.

**Nutritional Information per Serving:**
Calories: 372, carbs: 8g, fat: 17g, fiber: 2g, Protein: 47g, sodium: 808mg

## Pesto-Glazed Chicken Breasts

Preparation time: 5 minutes, Cooking time: 20 minutes, Serves: 4

Ingredients:
- ¼ cup of grated Parmesan cheese
- ¼ cup of pine nuts
- ¼ cup of plus 1 tbsp. of extra-virgin olive oil (divided)
- ¼ tsp. of black pepper (freshly ground)
- ½ tsp. of salt
- 1 garlic clove (minced)
- 1 packed cup of fresh basil leaves
- 4 chicken breasts (boneless & skinless)

Preparation:
1.      Heat 1 tbsp. of olive oil inside a large, heavy skillet placed over medium-high heat.

2.      Season both sides of the chicken breasts with pepper and salt then place them inside the skillet. Cook the first side for 10 minutes, then flip over and cook for another 5 minutes.

3.      In the meantime, mix the basil, Parmesan cheese, garlic, and pine nuts inside a food processor or blender, and blend on high. Pour in the leftover ¼ cup of olive oil gradually then blend it until smooth.

4.      Spread 1 tbsp. of pesto on every single chicken breast, then cover the skillet so it can cook for about 5 minutes. Serve the chicken pesto with its side up.

**Nutritional Information per Serving:**
Calories: 531, carbs: 2g, fat: 28g, fiber: 0g, Protein: 64g, sodium: 572mg

## Greek-Style Roast Turkey Breast

Preparation time: 10 minutes, Cooking time: 7½ hours, Serves: 8

Ingredients:
- ¼ tsp. of black pepper
- ¼ tsp. of cayenne pepper
- ¼ tsp. of ground nutmeg
- ½ cup of chicken stock
- ½ cup of oil-packed, sun-dried tomatoes (drained & thinly sliced)
- ½ cup of pitted kalamata olives
- ½ tsp. of ground cinnamon
- ½ tsp. of ground dill
- 1 (4-lb. / 1.8-kg) of turkey breast (trimmed of fat)
- 1 clove of garlic (minced)
- 1 tsp. of dried oregano
- 1 tsp. of sea salt
- 2 cups of chopped onions
- 2 tbsps. of fresh lemon juice
- 3 tbsps. of all-purpose flour

Preparation:

1.   Put the turkey breast, lemon juice, ¼ cup of chicken stock, onions, sun-dried tomatoes, Kalamata olives, and garlic into the slow cooker. Sprinkle the oregano, dill, cinnamon, nutmeg, black pepper, cayenne pepper, and salt over it. Cover it and cook for 7 hours on low.

2.   Mix the leftover ¼ cup of chicken stock and flour inside a small bowl. Whisk properly until smooth then stir the mixture into a slow cooker. Cover it and cook for an extra 30 minutes on low.

3.   Serve hot on rice, potatoes, pasta, or any other starch you prefer.

**Nutritional Information per Serving:**
Calories: 386, carbs: 8g, fat: 7g, fiber: 2g, Protein: 70g, sodium: 601mg

## Rosemary Baked Chicken Thighs

Preparation time: 20 minutes,| Cooking time: 20 minutes, Serves: 4 to 6

Ingredients:
- ¼ tsp. of black pepper (freshly ground)
- ⅓ cup of low-sodium chicken broth
- 1 lemon (juiced & zested)
- 1 rosemary sprig
- 2 to 2½ lb. (907 g to 1.1 kg) bone-in & skin-on chicken thighs (around 6 pieces)
- 2 tsps. of kosher salt
- 3 medium shallots (diced)
- 4 garlic cloves (peeled & crushed)
- 5 tbsps. of extra-virgin olive oil (divided)

Preparation:
1.    Heat 3 tbsps. of olive oil inside a large skillet or sauté pan placed over medium heat. Then include the garlic and shallots, and cook until fragrant for around 1 minute. Include the rosemary sprig.

2.    Use pepper and salt to season the chicken. Place it skin-side down inside the skillet and brown for about 3-5 minutes.

3.    When it's cooked about halfway through, flip the chicken then add the lemon juice and zest.

4.    Include the chicken broth then cover the pan and continue cooking for 10-15 additional minutes until the juices run clear and it is cooked through. Serve.

**Nutritional Information per Serving:**
Calories: 294, carbs: 3g, fat: 18g, fiber: 1g, Protein: 30g, sodium:
780mg

## Turkish Chicken Kebabs

Preparation time: 30 minutes, Cooking time: 15 minutes, Serves: 4

Ingredients:
- ¼ cup of plain Greek yogurt
- ½ tsp. of black pepper
- ½ tsp. of cayenne pepper
- ½ tsp. of ground cinnamon
- 1 lb. (454 g) of boneless & skinless chicken thighs (quartered crosswise)
- 1 tbsp. of fresh lemon juice
- 1 tbsp. of minced garlic
- 1 tbsp. of tomato paste
- 1 tbsp. of vegetable oil
- 1 tsp. of ground cumin
- 1 tsp. of kosher salt
- 1 tsp. of sweet Hungarian paprika

Preparation:
1.     Mix the yogurt, tomato paste, garlic, lemon juice, salt, vegetable oil, cumin, paprika, black pepper, cayenne, and cinnamon inside a big bowl. Stir well to blend the spices into the yogurt.

2.     Put the chicken into the bowl then toss well to coat. Marinate for 30 minutes at room temperature, then cover and place in a refrigerator for as much as 24 hours.

3.     Lay the chicken in 1 layer inside the air fryer basket. Then set the air fryer to 10 minutes at 375ºF or 191ºC. Flip the chicken over and cook for an additional 5 minutes. Using a meat thermometer, make sure the chicken's internal temperature reaches 165ºF or 74ºC.

**Nutritional Information per Serving:**
Calories: 188, carbs: 4g, fat: 8g, fiber: 1g, Protein: 24g, sodium: 705mg

## Cornish Hens with Honey-Lime Glaze

Preparation time: 15 minutes, Cooking time: 25 - 30 minutes, Serves: 2-3

Ingredients:
- 1 Cornish game hen (1½ to 2 lb. / 680 to 907 g)
- 1 tbsp. of honey
- 1 tbsp. of lime juice
- 1 tsp. of poultry seasoning
- Cooking spray
- Pepper (to taste)
- Salt (to taste)

Preparation:
1.     Split the hen into halves by cutting through the breast bone and then down one side of the hen's backbone.

2.     Combine the poultry seasoning, lime juice, and honey and rub or brush over all the hen's sides. Use pepper and salt to season to taste.

3.     Spray cooking spray over the air fryer basket and place the hen halves skin-side down inside the basket.

4.     Air fry for 25-30 minutes at 330ºF or 166ºC. The hen will only be done when the juices run clear after using a fork to pierce them at the leg joint. Allow the hen to rest for 5-10 minutes before you cut them.

**Nutritional Information per Serving:**
Calories: 287, carbs: 7g, fat: 8g, fiber: 0g, Protein: 46g, sodium: 155mg

# CHAPTER ELEVEN

## SALADS

### *Watermelon Burrata Salad*

Preparation time: 10 minutes, Cooking time: 0 minutes, Serves: 4

Ingredients:
- ¼ cup of balsamic vinegar
- ¼ cup of olive oil
- 1 tbsp. of lemon zest
- 1½ cups of small burrata cheese balls (cut into medium chunks)
- 2 cups of cubes or chunks of watermelon
- 2 shallots or 1 small red onion (thinly sliced into ½--moons)
- 4 fresh basil leaves sliced chiffonade-style (roll up basil leaves & slice into thin strips)
- Freshly ground black pepper (to taste)
- Salt (to taste)

Preparation:
1.    Mix all the ingredients inside a big bowl. Place in a refrigerator to chill before serving.

**Nutritional Information per Serving 1 cup:**
Calories: 224, carbs: 12g, fat: 14g, fiber: 1g, Protein: 14g, sodium: 560mg

## Cabbage and Carrot Salad

Preparation time: 10 minutes, Cooking time: 0 minutes, Serves: 3

Ingredients:
- ¼ tsp. of black pepper (freshly ground)
- ½ medium head cabbage (thinly sliced, rinsed, & drained)
- ½ tsp. of salt
- 1 garlic clove (minced)
- 3 medium carrots (peeled & shredded)
- 3 tbsps. of fresh lemon juice
- 4 tbsps. of extra virgin olive oil
- 8 Kalamata olives (pitted)

Preparation:

1.    Place the carrots and cabbage inside a big bowl then toss.

2.    Mix the olive oil, black pepper, lemon juice, salt, and garlic inside a small bowl or jar. Shake or whisk to combine.

3.    Pour the mixture/dressing over the salad then toss. (Note: Its volume will reduce)

4.    Scatter the olives all over the salad before serving. Store it, covered inside the fridge for about 2 days.

**Nutritional Information per Serving:**
Calories: 237, carbs: 16g, fat: 19g, fiber: 6g, Protein: 3g, sodium: 570mg

## Tossed Green Mediterranean Salad

Preparation time: 15 minutes, Cooking time: 0 minutes, Serves: 4

Ingredients:
- ¼ tsp. of fine sea salt
- ⅓ cup of extra virgin olive oil
- ½ cup of fresh dill (finely chopped)
- 1 medium head of romaine lettuce (washed, dried, & chopped to bite-sized pieces)
- 2 medium cucumbers (peeled & sliced)
- 2 tbsps. of fresh lemon juice
- 3 spring onions (only the white parts) (sliced)
- 4 oz. (113 g) of crumbled feta
- 7 Kalamata olives (pitted)

Preparation:
1.     Add the dill, spring onions, cucumber, and lettuce to a big bowl. Toss to mix.

2.     Whisk the lemon juice and olive oil together inside a small bowl. Pour the dressing on the salad, then toss, and sprinkle the sea salt on top.

3.     Sprinkle the olives and feta on top and toss the salad gently once more. Serve immediately. (It's best to serve this recipe fresh.)

**Nutritional Information per Serving:**
Calories: 284, carbs: 10g, fat: 25g, fiber: 5g, Protein: 7g, sodium: 496mg

## Taverna-Style Greek Salad

Preparation time: 20 minutes, Cooking time: 0 minutes, Serves: 4

Ingredients:
- ¼ cup of capers (or more olives)
- ½ cup of extra-virgin olive oil (divided into 1 of pack feta cheese)
- 1 large cucumber (peeled & roughly chopped)
- 1 medium-sized green bell pepper (sliced)
- 1 small red onion (sliced)
- 1 tsp. of dried oregano (or any fresh herbs you prefer, such as cilantro, parsley, basil, or chives; divided)
- 4-5 medium tomatoes (roughly chopped)
- 16 pitted Kalamata olives
- Optional: salt, fresh oregano, and pepper (for garnish)

Preparation:

1.     Put the vegetables inside a big serving bowl. Then add the feta, ½ the olive oil, olives, capers, and ½ the dried oregano. Mix well to combine.

2.     Put the entire feta cheese piece on top, sprinkle with the leftover dried oregano, then drizzle over with the leftover olive oil.

3.     Season to your taste and serve instantly, or store inside the refrigerator for about a day.

**Nutritional Information per Serving:**
Calories: 320, carbs: 11g, fat: 31g, fiber: 4g, Protein: 3g, sodium: 445mg

## *Marinated Greek Salad with Oregano and Goat Cheese*

Preparation time: 10 minutes, Cooking time: 0 minutes, Serves: 4

Ingredients:
- ¼ tsp. of black pepper (freshly ground)
- ½ cup of white wine vinegar
- ½ tsp. of salt
- 1 medium red onion (cut into rings)
- 1 pint of mixed small heirloom tomatoes (halved)
- 1 small garlic clove (minced)
- 1 tsp. of crumbled Greek oregano (dried)
- 2 oz. (57 g) of feta or crumbled goat cheese
- 2 Persian cucumbers (sliced thinly)
- 4-6 skinny, long yellow or red banana peppers (or other mild peppers)

Preparation:

1.    In a big, nonreactive (glass, plastic, or ceramic) bowl, whisk the vinegar, oregano, garlic, pepper, and salt together. Add the peppers, cucumbers, and onion then toss well to mix. Cover and place in the fridge for a minimum of 1 hour.

2.    Put the tomatoes inside the bowl then toss well to coat. Top with the cheese and serve.

**Nutritional Information per Serving:**
Calories: 98, carbs: 13g, fat: 4g, fiber: 3g, Protein: 4g, sodium: 460mg

## *Italian Tuna and Olive Salad*

Preparation time: 5 minutes, Cooking time: 0 minutes, Serves: 4

Ingredients:
- ¼ cup of olive oil
- 1 cup of pitted green olives
- 1 medium red bell pepper (seeded & diced)
- 1 small clove of garlic (minced)
- 1 tsp. of salt
- 2 (6-oz. / 170-g) jars or cans of tuna in olive oil (well drained)
- 3 tbsps. of white wine vinegar
- Several leaves of curly green (or red lettuce)

Preparation:

1.  Whisk the olive oil, salt, and vinegar together inside a big bowl.

2.  Add the bell pepper, garlic, and olives to the dressing then toss to coat. Add the tuna, stir, cover, and let it chill inside the fridge for not less than an hour to allow the flavors to blend.

3.  To serve, use the lettuce leaves to line a serving bowl then top with the salad. Serve chilled.

**Nutritional Information per Serving:**
Calories: 339, carbs: 4g, fat: 24g, fiber: 2g, Protein: 25g, sodium: 626mg

# Arugula and Fennel Salad with Fresh Basil

Preparation time: 5 minutes, Cooking time: 0 minutes, Serves: 4

Ingredients:
- ¼ cup of julienned fresh basil leaves
- ¼ cup of toasted pine nuts
- ½ cup of crumbled feta cheese
- ½ tsp. of salt
- 1 medium bulb fennel (very thinly sliced)
- 1 small cucumber (very thinly sliced)
- 1 teaspoon honey
- 2 cups of arugula
- 3 tbsps. of lemon juice
- 3 tbsps. of olive oil

Preparation:
1.    Whisk the lemon juice, olive oil, salt, and honey together inside a medium bowl. Add the cucumber and fennel then coat by tossing before allowing it to sit for about 10 minutes.

2.    Place the arugula inside a big salad bowl. Include the fennel, marinated cucumber, and the dressing in the salad bowl and toss properly. Sprinkle with feta cheese, pine nuts, and basil then serve instantly.

Nutritional Information per Serving:
Calories: 237, carbs: 11g, fat: 21g, fiber: 3g, Protein: 6g, sodium: 537mg

## Greek Village Salad

Preparation time: 10 minutes, Cooking time: 0 minutes, Serves: 4

Ingredients:

- ¼ cup of extra-virgin olive oil (add extra for drizzling)
- ¼ lemon
- ¼ tsp. of dried oregano (add extra for garnish)
- 1 cup of kalamata olives (for topping)
- 1 English cucumber (peeled & cut into medium chunks)
- 2 green bell peppers (cut into medium chunks)
- 2 red onions (sliced or cut into medium chunks)
- 4 oz. (113 g) of Greek feta cheese (sliced)
- 5 large tomatoes (cut into medium chunks)

Preparation:

1. Mix the cucumber, olive oil, tomatoes, onions, bell peppers, oregano, and olives inside a big bowl.

2. Evenly split the vegetable mixture between 4 bowls then top every single one with a slice of feta and a squirt of lemon juice. Drizzle olive oil over it, garnish with the oregano, then serve.

**Nutritional Information per Serving:**
Calories: 315, carbs: 1121g, fat: 24g, fiber: 6g, Protein: 8g, sodium: 524mg

## *Wilted Kale Salad*

Preparation time: 10 minutes, Cooking time: 5 minutes, Serves: 4

Ingredients:
- 1 cup of cherry tomatoes (sliced)
- 1 tbsp. of olive oil (add 1 teaspoon extra)
- 2 cloves of garlic (minced)
- 2 heads of kale
- Freshly ground pepper (to taste)
- Juice of 1 lemon
- Sea salt (to taste)

Preparation:
1.    Rinse the kale and dry it.

2.    Rip the kale into small bite-sized pieces.

3.    Heat 1 tbsp. of the olive oil inside a large skillet, then add the garlic and cook for a minute before adding the kale.

4.    Cook until just wilted, then include the tomatoes.

5.    Cook until the tomatoes get soft, then take it off the heat.

6.    Put the kale and tomatoes inside a bowl, then season with freshly ground pepper and sea salt.

7.    Drizzle the leftover lemon juice and olive oil over it and serve.

**Nutritional Information per Serving:**
Calories: 153, carbs: 23g, fat: 6g, fiber: 9g, Protein: 10g, sodium: 88mg

## *Tricolor Tomato Summer Salad*

Preparation time: 10 minutes, Cooking time: 0 minutes, Serves: 3-4

Ingredients:
- ¼ cup of crumbled feta (optional)
- ¼ cup of extra-virgin olive oil
- ¼ cup of white balsamic vinegar
- ½ cucumber (peeled & diced)
- ½ tsp. of black pepper (freshly ground)
- ½ tsp. of garlic salt
- 1 small red onion (thinly sliced)
- 1 tbsp. of sugar
- 1½ cups of chopped tomatoes (yellow, orange, and red)
- 2 tbsps. of Dijon mustard

Preparation:

1.    Whisk the mustard, vinegar, sugar, garlic, pepper, and salt inside a small bowl. Then whisk the olive oil in slowly.

2.    Put the cucumber, tomatoes, and red onion inside a big bowl. Add the dressing and toss one or two times. Serve, topped with feta crumbles (if using).

Nutritional Information per Serving:
Calories: 246, carbs: 19g, fat: 18g, fiber: 2g, Protein: 1g, sodium: 483mg

# CHAPTER TWELVE

# SNACKS & APPETIZERS

## *Sweet Potato Hummus*

Preparation time: 10 minutes, Cooking time: 1 hour, Serves: 8-10

Ingredients:
- 1 (15-oz. / 425-g) can of chickpeas (drained)
- 1 lb. (454 g) of sweet potatoes (around 2)
- 1 tsp. of Aleppo pepper or red pepper flakes
- 2 tbsps. of fresh lemon juice
- 2 tbsps. of olive oil
- 2 tsps. of ground cumin
- 4 garlic cloves (minced)
- Pita bread, pita chips, or fresh vegetables (for serving)

Preparation:
1.    Let the oven preheat to 400°F or 205°C.

2.    Prick a few places on the sweet potatoes with a small, sharp knife then line them on top of a baking sheet. Roast for about 1 hour until thoroughly cooked, then set them aside to cool afterward, peel the sweet potatoes and place the flesh inside a food processor or blender.

3.    Include the chickpeas, cumin, garlic, olive oil, $1/3$ cup water, and lemon juice. Blend till smooth before adding the Aleppo pepper.

4.    Serve with pita bread and pita chips.

**Nutritional Information per Serving:**
Calories: 178, carbs: 30g, fat: 5g, fiber: 9g, Protein: 7g, sodium: 149mg

# Roasted Rosemary Olives

Preparation time: 5 minutes, Cooking time: 25 minutes, Serves: 4

Ingredients:
- 1 cup of mixed variety olives (pitted & rinsed)
- 1 tbsp. of extra-virgin olive oil
- 2 tbsps. of lemon juice
- 4 rosemary sprigs
- 6 garlic cloves (peeled)

Preparation:

1.    Let the oven preheat to 400ºF or 205ºC. Then use foil or parchment paper to line the baking sheet.

2.    Mix the olives, olive oil, lemon juice, and garlic inside a medium bowl. Then spread it in a single layer on top of the already prepared baking sheet. Sprinkle the rosemary on top and roast for about 25 minutes, and toss it halfway through.

3.    Take the rosemary leaves out of the stem and put them inside a serving bowl. Then include the olives, then mix before you serve.

## Nutritional Information per Serving:
Calories: 100, carbs: 4g, fat: 9g, fiber: 0g, Protein: 0g, sodium: 260mg

## *Baked Eggplant Baba Ganoush*

Preparation time: 10 minutes, Cooking time: 1 hour, Makes: around 4 cups

Ingredients:
- ½ tsp. of ground sumac, add more for sprinkling (optional)
- ¾ tsp. of kosher salt
- 1 tbsp. of extra-virgin olive oil
- 1/3 cup of fresh parsley (chopped)
- 2 lb. (907 g, approximately 2 medium-large) eggplant
- 2 tbsps. of lemon juice
- 3 tbsps. of tahini
- Zest of 1 lemon

Preparation:
1. Let the oven preheat to 350ºF or 180ºC. Lay the eggplants right on the rack then bake for sixty minutes, or just until the skin becomes wrinkly.

2. Put the lemon juice, tahini, lemon zest, sumac, and salt inside a food processor. Cut the baked eggplant open very carefully and put the flesh in the food processor. Process until well blended.

3. Place it inside a serving dish then add the parsley and mix. Drizzle the olive oil over it then sprinkle with the sumac (if needed).

**Nutritional Information per Serving:**
Calories: 50, carbs: 2g, fat: 16g, fiber: 1g, Protein: 4g, sodium: 110mg

# Warm Olives with Rosemary and Garlic

Preparation time: 5 minutes, Cooking time: 3 minutes, Serves: 4

Ingredients:
- ¼ tsp. of salt
- 1 clove of garlic (chopped)
- 1 cup of whole cured black olives (such as Kalamata)
- 1 tbsp. of olive oil
- 2 sprigs of fresh rosemary

Preparation:

1. Heat the olive oil inside a medium-sized saucepan on medium heat. Then add the rosemary, garlic, and salt. Decrease to low heat and cook for 1 minute, stirring continuously.

2. Add the olives then cook for approximately 2 minutes, stirring occasionally till the olives get warm.

3. For serving, use a slotted spoon to scoop the olives out of the pan into the serving bowl. Then pour the garlic and rosemary on the olives. Serve warm.

**Nutritional Information per Serving:**
Calories: 71, carbs: 3g, fat: 7g, fiber: 1g, Protein: 1g, sodium: 441mg

# Seared Halloumi with Pesto and Tomato

Preparation time: 2 minutes, Cooking time: 5 minutes, Serves: 2

Ingredients:
- 1 medium tomato (sliced)
- 2 tsps. of prepared pesto sauce (add more for drizzling as desired)
- 3 oz. (85 g) of Halloumi cheese (cut the crosswise into 2 thin, rectangular pieces)

Preparation:
1.	Heat the nonstick skillet on medium-high heat then place the Halloumi slices inside the hot pan. After approximately 2 minutes, check to ensure the bottom of the cheese is golden. If it's golden, flip each slice, and everyone one with 1 tsp. of pesto, then cook for additional 2 minutes, or just until the other side turns golden.

2.	Serve with the tomato slices and a drizzle of the pesto on the side, if preferred.

**Nutritional Information per Serving:**
Calories: 177, carbs: 4g, fat: 14g, fiber: 1g, Protein: 10g, sodium: 233mg

## Lemony Olives and Feta Medley

Preparation time: 10 minutes, Cooking time: 0 minutes, Serves: 8

Ingredients:
- ¼ cup of extra-virgin olive oil
- 1 (1-lb. / 454-g) block of Greek feta cheese
- 1 tsp. of dried oregano
- 1 tsp. of lemon zest (grated)
- 3 cups of mixed olives (Kalamata & green); drained from the brine; (preferably pitted)
- 3 tbsps. of lemon juice
- Pita bread (for serving)

Preparation:

1.    Chop the feta cheese into ½" squares then place them in a big bowl.

2.    Put the olives in the feta then set it aside.

3.    Whisk the lemon juice, olive oil, oregano, and lemon zest together inside a small bowl.

4.    Pour the dressing on top of the olives and feta cheese then toss gently together to coat everything evenly.

5.    Serve alongside pita bread.

**Nutritional Information per Serving:**
Calories: 269, carbs: 6g, fat: 24g, fiber: 2g, Protein: 9g, sodium: 891mg

## *Creamy Traditional Hummus*

Preparation time: 5 minutes, Cooking time: 0 minutes, Serves: 8

Ingredients:
- ¼ cup of lemon juice
- ¼ cup of plain Greek yogurt
- ½ cup of tahini paste
- 1 (15-oz. / 425-g) can of garbanzo beans (rinsed & drained)
- 1 tsp. of salt
- 2 cloves of garlic (peeled)
- 2 tbsps. of extra-virgin olive oil (divided)

Preparation:
1.    Put the garbanzo beans, lemon juice, garlic cloves, and salt inside a food processor with a chopping blade fitted to it. Blend until smooth for about a minute.

2.    Scrape down all the sides of the food processor. Then add the tahini paste, Greek yogurt, & 1 tbsp. of olive oil. Blend for an additional minute, until it is creamy and well mixed.

3.    Transfer the hummus to a serving bowl, then drizzle the leftover tbsp. of olive oil over it.

**Nutritional Information per Serving:**
Calories: 189, carbs: 14g, fat: 13g, fiber: 4g, Protein: 7g, sodium: 313mg

## Honey-Rosemary Almonds

Preparation time: 5 minutes, Cooking time: 10 minutes, Serves: 6

Ingredients:
- ¼ tsp. of kosher or sea salt
- 1 cup of whole, shelled almonds (raw)
- 1 tbsp. of honey
- 1 tbsp. of minced fresh rosemary
- Nonstick cooking spray

Preparation:

1.    Mix the rosemary, almonds, and salt inside a big skillet placed over medium heat. Frequently stir it for 1 minute.

2.    Drizzle the honey into the mixture and cook for an additional 3-4 minutes, stirring often, till the almonds are well coated and only beginning to darken around the edges.

3.    Take it off the heat. Use a spatula to spread the almonds on a pan already coated with the nonstick cooking spray. Let it cool for about 10 minutes, then break the almonds up before serving.

**Nutritional Information per Serving:**
Calories: 149, carbs: 8g, fat: 12g, fiber: 3g, Protein: 5g, sodium: 97mg

## *Taste of the Mediterranean Fat Bombs*

Preparation time: 15 minutes, Cooking time: 0 minutes, Makes: 6 fat bombs

Ingredients:
- ½ cup of walnuts (finely chopped)
- 1 cup of crumbled goat cheese
- 1 tbsp. of fresh rosemary (chopped)
- 4 tbsps. of jarred pesto
- 12 pitted Kalamata olives (finely chopped)

Preparation:
1. Mix the goat cheese, olives, and pesto inside a medium-sized bowl, and use a fork to mix it properly. Refrigerate for a minimum of 4 hours to allow it to harden.

2. Use your hands to mold the mixture into 6 balls, around ¾" in diameter. The mixture will get sticky.

3. Keep the rosemary and walnuts inside a small bowl, then coat the goat cheese balls inside the nut mixture by rolling it.

4. Refrigerate the fat bombs for about a week or store them inside the freezer for as long as 1 month.

**Nutritional Information per Serving (1 fat bomb):**
Calories: 235, carbs: 2g, fat: 22g, fiber: 1g, Protein: 10g, sodium: 365mg

## Salmon-Stuffed Cucumbers

Preparation time: 10 minutes, Cooking time: 0 minutes, Serves: 4

Ingredients:
- 2 large cucumbers, peeled
- 1 (4-ounce / 113-g) can of red salmon
- 1 medium very ripe avocado, peeled, pitted, and mashed
- 1 tablespoon extra-virgin olive oil
- Zest and juice of 1 lime
- 3 tablespoons chopped fresh cilantro
- ½ teaspoon salt
- ¼ teaspoon freshly ground black pepper

Preparation:

1.   Cut the cucumber into 1"-thick sections then use a spoon to scrape seeds from each segment's center and let it stand on a plate.

2.   Mix the salmon, olive oil, avocado, lime zest and juice, pepper, salt, and cilantro inside a medium-sized bowl. Keep mixing until creamy.

3.   Spoon out the salmon mixture into each cucumber segment's center and serve chilled.

**Nutritional Information per Serving:**
Calories: 173, carbs: 8g, fat: 13g, fiber: 4g, Protein: 8g, sodium: 420mg

# CHAPTER THIRTEEN

# STAPLES, SAUCES, DIPS, & DRESSINGS

### *Red Gazpacho*

Preparation time: 15 minutes, Cooking time: 0 minutes, Serves: 4

Ingredients:
- ¼ cup of fresh chives (chopped, for garnish)
- ¼ tsp. of black pepper (freshly ground)
- ½ tsp. of kosher salt
- ¹/₃ cup of extra-virgin olive oil
- 1 bell pepper (cut into chunks)
- 1 cucumber (cut into chunks)
- 1 garlic clove (smashed)
- 1 small red onion (cut into chunks)
- 2 lb. (907 g) of tomatoes (cut into chunks)
- 2 tsps. of sherry vinegar
- Lemon juice (optional)

Preparation:
1.    Put the tomatoes, cucumber, bell pepper, onion, vinegar, garlic, black pepper, and salt inside a high-speed blender or a Vitamix. Blend until very smooth. While the motor is still running, pour in the olive oil then purée until very smooth.

2.    Add a spritz of lemon juice or more vinegar as desired. Use the chives to garnish and serve.

**Nutritional Information per Serving:**
Calories: 140, carbs: 18g, fat: 19g, fiber: 5g, Protein: 4g, sodium: 155mg

## Spicy Carrot-Orange Soup

Preparation time: 15 minutes, Cooking time: 35 minutes, Serves: 6

Ingredients:
- 1 lb. (454 g) of carrots (coarsely chopped; 2½ cups)
- 1 small onion (chopped; approximately 1 cup)
- 1 tbsp. of Aleppo pepper
- 1 tsp. of salt
- 2 garlic cloves (chopped)
- 2 tbsps. of Greek yogurt (optional)
- 2 tbsps. of olive oil
- 4 cups of chicken broth or vegetable broth (no-salt-added)
- Zest & juice of 1 orange (approximately 1 tbsp. of zest & ⅓ cup of juice)

Preparation:
1.    In a large saucepan, heat the oil over medium heat. Add the onion and cook until starting to soften but not brown, 7 to 8 minutes.

2.    Add the garlic and cook for 1 minute, or until fragrant.

3.    Add the broth, carrots, orange zest, orange juice, and Aleppo pepper; bring to a boil. Reduce the heat to maintain a simmer and cook for 20 to 25 minutes, until the vegetables are tender.

4.    Using a hand blender (or a regular blender, working in batches), blend the soup until smooth.

5.    Ladle the soup into bowls, top with a little yogurt, if desired, and serve.

**Nutritional Information per Serving (1 cup):**
Calories: 125, carbs: 18g, fat: 5g, fiber: 6g, Protein: 3g, sodium: 467mg

## Turkish Red Lentil Bride Soup

Preparation time: 5 minutes, Cooking time: 55 minutes, Serves: 4

Ingredients:
- ¼ cup of fresh mint (chopped)
- ⅓ cup of bulgur wheat
- ½ cup of red lentils (rinsed)
- ½ tsp. of hot paprika (add more to taste)
- 1 quart of low-sodium vegetable broth or chicken broth
- 1 tbsp. of tomato paste
- 1 yellow onion (finely chopped)
- 2 tbsps. of fresh lemon juice
- 2 tbsps. of olive oil
- Kosher salt (to taste)

Preparation:

1.     Warm the oil inside a big saucepan and place over medium heat until it shimmers. Cook the onion for approximately 10 minutes, stirring continuously until golden.

2.     Stir in the bulgur, lentils, and paprika to coat well in the oil. Include the tomato paste and, stirring, cook for approximately 2 minutes till the color gets dark.

3.     Include the broth then allow it to boil. Decrease the heat till it gets to a simmer then, stirring irregularly to prevent sticking, cook for approximately 40 minutes until the bulgur and lentils are creamy and tender.

4.     Stir in the lemon juice and mint. Season with salt to taste.

**Nutritional Information per Serving:**
Calories: 206, carbs: 27g, fat: 8g, fiber: 7g, Protein: 9g, sodium: 139mg

## Chickpea Stew

Preparation time: 10 minutes, Cooking time: 6-8 hours, Serves: 6

Ingredients:
- ¼ tsp. of black pepper (freshly ground)
- ½ tsp. of ground coriander
- ½ tsp. of sea salt
- 1 green bell pepper (seeded & chopped)
- 1 small onion (diced)
- 1 tbsp. of drained capers
- 1 tbsp. of extra-virgin olive oil
- 1 tsp. of ground cumin
- 1 tsp. of ground turmeric
- 2 cups of dried chickpeas (rinsed)
- 2 garlic cloves (minced)
- 4 cups of chicken broth or vegetable broth (low-sodium)

Preparation:

1.    Mix the chickpeas, olive oil, vegetable broth, onion, garlic, bell pepper, capers, turmeric, cumin, coriander, black pepper, and salt inside a slow cooker. Stir until well mixed.

2.    Cover and cook on low heat for 6-8 hours.

**Nutritional Information per Serving:**
Calories: 286, carbs: 45g, fat: 6g, fiber: 13g, Protein: 14g, sodium: 347mg

## *Greek Salad Soup*

Preparation time: 15 minutes, Cooking time: 6-8 hours, Serves: 6

Ingredients:
- ½ tsp. of black pepper (freshly ground)
- 1 cup of whole Kalamata olives (pitted)
- 1 small red onion (diced)
- 1 tbsp. of extra-virgin olive oil
- 1 tsp. of sea salt
- 1½ tsps. of dried oregano
- 2 cucumbers (cut into 1"-thick rounds)
- 2 cups of water
- 2 green bell peppers (seeded & diced)
- 2 tsps. of red wine vinegar
- 4 cups of chicken broth (low-sodium)
- 4 oz. (113 g) of feta cheese (crumbled)
- 4 tomatoes (cut into wedges)

Preparation:

1.    Mix the tomatoes, bell peppers, cucumbers, onion, chicken broth, olives, water, vinegar, olive oil, oregano, black pepper, and salt inside a slow cooker. Stir until well mixed.

2.    Cover and cook on low heat for 6-8 hours.

3.    Top every single bowl with feta cheese then serve.

**Nutritional Information per Serving:**
Calories: 180, carbs: 13g, fat: 12g, fiber: 3g, Protein: 6g, sodium: 976mg

## *Mediterranean Vegetable Soup*

Preparation time: 20 minutes, Cooking time: 6-8 hours, Serves: 6

Ingredients:
- ½ tsp. of black pepper (freshly ground)
- 1 (28-oz. / 794-g) can of diced tomatoes (no-salt-added)
- 1 green bell pepper (seeded & chopped)
- 1 small red onion (chopped)
- 1 tbsp. of extra-virgin olive oil
- 1 tsp. of paprika
- 1 tsp. of sea salt
- 1 yellow or red bell pepper (seeded & chopped)
- 2 cups of vegetable broth (low-sodium)
- 2 tsps. of dried oregano
- 2 zucchini (chopped)
- 3 garlic cloves (minced)
- 4 oz. (113 g) of mushrooms (sliced)
- Juice of 1 lemon

Preparation:

1.    Mix the tomatoes, red and green bell peppers, vegetable broth, mushrooms, onion, zucchini, garlic, oregano, olive oil, paprika, black pepper, and salt inside a slow cooker. Stir until well mixed.

2.    Cover and cook on low heat for 6-8 hours.

3.    Add the lemon juice and stir before serving.

**Nutritional Information per Serving:**
Calories: 91, carbs: 16g, fat: 3g, fiber: 5g, Protein: 3g, sodium: 502mg

# Lentil Soup with Spinach

Preparation time: 5 minutes, Cooking time: 20 minutes, Serves: 6

Ingredients:
- 1 cup of onion (chopped)
- 1 tbsp. of curry powder
- 1 tsp. of olive oil
- 1½ cups of lentils
- 6 cups of water
- 12 oz. (340 g) of spinach

Preparation:

1.    Heat the olive oil then add the onion to sauté. Add the curry powder and lentils. Stir well.

2.    Pour in the water and cook for approximately 15 to 20 minutes, until lentils get tender. Add the spinach then stir until it wilts.

3.    Serve alongside a green salad and toasted whole-wheat bread.

**Nutritional Information per Serving:**
Calories: 48, carbs: 9g, fat: 1g, fiber: 3g, Protein: 4g, sodium: 53mg

# Cold Cucumber Soup

Preparation time: 10 minutes, Cooking time: 0 minutes, Serves: 4

Ingredients:
- ½ cup of mint (finely chopped)
- 1 tbsp. of tomato paste
- 2 cups of plain Greek yogurt
- 2 cups of vegetable stock or chicken broth
- 2 garlic cloves (minced)
- 2 seedless cucumbers (peeled & cut into chunks)
- 3 tsps. of fresh dill
- Freshly ground pepper (to taste)
- Sea salt (to taste)

Preparation:

1.    Purée the yogurt, cucumber, garlic, and mint inside a blender or food processor.

2.    Add the dill, chicken broth, tomato paste, pepper, and sea salt then blend wholly.

3.    Place in a refrigerator for a minimum of 2 hours before you serve.

**Nutritional Information per Serving:**
Calories: 119, carbs: 12g, fat: 5g, fiber: 2g, Protein: 8g, sodium: 98mg

## Creamy Tomato Hummus Soup

Preparation time: 10 minutes, Cooking time: 10 minutes, Serves: 2

Ingredients:
- ¼ cup of fresh basil leaves (thinly sliced; optional: for garnish)
- 1 (14½-oz. / 411-g) can of crushed tomatoes with basil
- 1 cup of red pepper hummus (roasted)
- 2 cups of chicken stock (low-sodium)
- Garlic croutons (optional: for garnish)
- Salt

Preparation:
1.    Mix the chicken stock, hummus, and canned tomatoes inside a blender then blend till very smooth. Transfer the mixture to a saucepan then bring to a boil.

2.    Season with fresh basil and salt if preferred. Garnish with garlic croutons and serve, if preferred.

**Nutritional Information per Serving:**
Calories: 148, carbs: 19g, fat: 6g, fiber: 4g, Protein: 5g, sodium: 680mg

## Cranberry Bean Minestrone

Preparation time: 15 minutes, Cooking time: 3 hours, 30 minutes, Serves: 6

Ingredients:
- ½ tsp. of ground black pepper
- ½ tsp. of kosher salt
- 1 (14½-oz. / 411-g) can of diced tomatoes

- 1 bay leaf
- 1 onion (chopped)
- 1 quart of vegetable broth (low-sodium)
- 1 small zucchini (halved lengthwise & sliced ¼-inch thick)
- 1 tbsp. of dried oregano
- 1½ cups of whole grain ditalini (or elbow pasta)
- 2 (15-oz. / 425-g) cans of cranberry beans (drained & rinsed)
- 2 carrots (thinly sliced)
- 2 ribs of celery (thinly sliced)
- 3 cloves of garlic (sliced)
- 3 tbsps. of fresh basil (shredded)
- 6 tbsps. of Parmigiano-Reggiano cheese (finely grated)

Preparation:

1. Mix the broth, carrots, tomatoes, celery, garlic, onion, oregano, pepper, salt, and bay leaf inside a 4- or 6-quart slow cooker. Then cover and cook for 3-4 hours on high or 6-8 hours on low until the vegetables get tender.

2. Take off the cover then add the pasta, zucchini, and beans. Cook for approximately 30 minutes on high until the pasta becomes tender. Take out the bay leaf and then use the basil and cheese to garnish each serving.

**Nutritional Information per Serving:**
Calories: 321, carbs: 59g, fat: 4g, fiber: 7g, Protein: 14g, sodium: 857mg

# CHAPTER FOURTEEN

# VEGETABLES & SIDES

### *Citrus-Roasted Broccoli Florets*

Preparation time: 5 minutes, Cooking time: 12 minutes, Serves: 6

Ingredients:
- ½ cup of orange juice
- ½ tsp. of salt
- 1 tbsp. of raw honey
- 2 tbsps. of olive oil
- 4 cups of broccoli florets (around 1 large head)
- Orange wedges (optional), for serving

Preparation:
1.    Let the air fryer preheat to 360°F or 182°C.

2.    Mix the orange juice, broccoli, olive oil, honey, and salt inside a big bowl. Toss in the broccoli until it is well coated.

3.    Transfer the broccoli mixture to the air fryer basket then let it roast for 6 minutes. Stir then roast for an additional 6 minutes.

4.    Serve alone or, for extra citrus flavor, with orange wedges (if desired).

**Nutritional Information per Serving:**
Calories: 73, carbs: 8g, fat: 5g, fiber: 0g, Protein: 2g, sodium: 207mg

## Roasted Grape Tomatoes and Asparagus

Preparation time: 5 minutes, Cooking time: 12 minutes, Serves: 6

Ingredients:

- ½ tsp. of kosher salt
- 1 bunch of asparagus (trimmed)
- 2 cups of grape tomatoes
- 2 tbsps. of olive oil
- 3 garlic cloves (minced)

Preparation:

1. Let the air fryer preheat to 380°F.

2. Mix all the ingredients inside a big bowl, tossing to coat all the vegetables with the oil.

3. Add the vegetable mixture to the air fryer basket then spread in a single layer and roast for about 12 minutes.

### Nutritional Information per Serving:

Calories: 56, carbs: 3g, fat: 5g, fiber: 1g, Protein: 1g, sodium: 197mg

## Parmesan and Herb Sweet Potatoes

Preparation time: 10 minutes, Cooking time: 18 minutes, Serves: 4

Ingredients:

- ¼ cup of olive oil
- ½ tsp. of salt
- 1 tsp. of dried rosemary
- 2 large sweet potatoes (peeled & cubed)
- 2 tbsps. of shredded Parmesan

Preparation:

1.    Let the air fryer preheat to 360ºF or 182ºC.

2.    Toss the sweet potatoes in a big bowl along with the rosemary, olive oil, and salt.

3.    Add the potatoes to the air fryer basket then roast for around 10 minutes, then stir and sprinkle the Parmesan on top. Keep roasting for an additional 8 minutes.

4.    Serve hot.

**Nutritional Information per Serving:**
Calories: 186, carbs: 13g, fat: 14g, fiber: 2g, Protein: 2g, sodium: 369mg

## Roasted Radishes with Sea Salt

Preparation time: 5 minutes, Cooking time: 18 minutes, Serves: 4

Ingredients:
- ½ tsp. of sea salt
- 1 lb. (454 g) of radishes (ends trimmed if required)
- 2 tbsps. of olive oil

Preparation:

1.   Let the air fryer preheat to 360ºF or 182ºC.

2.   Mix radishes along with the sea salt and olive oil inside a big bowl.

3.   Transfer the radishes to the air fryer and let them roast for 10 minutes. Turn or stir the radishes over then roast for an additional 8 minutes.

4.   Serve.

**Nutritional Information per Serving:**
Calories: 80, carbs: 5g, fat: 7g, fiber: 2g, Protein: 1g, sodium: 315mg

## Garlicky Sautéed Zucchini with Mint

Preparation time: 5 minutes, Cooking time: 10 minutes, Serves: 4

Ingredients:
- 1 large onion (chopped)
- 1 tsp. of dried mint
- 1 tsp. of salt
- 3 cloves of garlic (minced)

- 3 large green zucchini
- 3 tbsps. of extra-virgin olive oil

Preparation:

1. Chop the zucchini into ½" cubes.

2. Cook the olive oil, garlic, and onions for 3 minutes inside a big skillet placed over medium heat, stirring continually.

3. Put the salt and zucchini into the skillet then toss well to mix with the garlic and onions. Cook for 5 minutes.

4. Add the mint and toss to combine. Let it cook for an additional 2 minutes. Serve warm.

**Nutritional Information per Serving:**
Calories: 147, carbs: 12g, fat: 11g, fiber: 3g, Protein: 4g, sodium: 607mg

### *Rustic Cauliflower and Carrot Hash*

Preparation time: 10 minutes, Cooking time: 10 minutes, Serves: 4

Ingredients:
- ½ tsp. of ground cumin
- 1 large onion (chopped)
- 1 tbsp. of garlic (minced)
- 1 tsp. of salt
- 2 cups of carrots (diced)
- 3 tbsps. of extra-virgin olive oil
- 4 cups of cauliflower pieces (washed)

Preparation:
1.    Cook the olive oil, carrots, garlic, and onion for 3 minutes inside a big skillet placed over medium heat.

2.    Chop the cauliflower into bite-size or 1-inch pieces. Add the cumin, salt, and cauliflower to the skillet then toss to mix with the onions and carrots.

3.    Cover the skillet and cook for up to 3 minutes.

4.    Toss the veggies and keep cooking uncovered for 3-4 minutes more.

5.    Serve warm.

**Nutritional Information per Serving:**
Calories: 159, carbs: 15g, fat: 11g, fiber: 5g, Protein: 3g, sodium: 657mg

### *Mediterranean Lentil Sloppy Joes*
Preparation time: 5 minutes, Cooking time: 15 minutes, Serves: 4

Ingredients:
- ¼ tsp. of kosher or sea salt
- 1 (14½-oz. / 411-g) can of no-salt-added or low-sodium diced tomatoes (undrained)
- 1 (15-oz. / 425-g) can of lentils (drained & rinsed)
- 1 cup of chopped bell pepper of any color (approximately 1 medium bell pepper)
- 1 cup of chopped onion (approximately ½ medium onion)
- 1 cup of romaine lettuce (chopped)

- 1 tbsp. of extra-virgin olive oil
- 1 tsp. of dried thyme
- 1 tsp. of ground cumin
- 1½ cups of chopped, seedless cucumber (1 medium cucumber)
- 2 minced garlic cloves (approximately 1 tsp.)
- 4 whole-wheat pita bread (split open)

Preparation:

1. Heat the oil inside a medium-sized saucepan placed over medium-high heat.

2. Add the bell pepper and onion and, stirring often, cook for up to 4 minutes.

3. Add the garlic then, stirring often, and cook for a minute. Add the tomatoes (with their liquid), lentils, thyme, cumin, and salt. Reduce the heat to medium then cook for 10 minutes, stirring occasionally, until almost all the liquid evaporates.

4. Stuff the mixture of lentils into each pita. Lay the lettuce and cucumbers on the lentil mixture.

5. Serve.

**Nutritional Information per Serving:**
Calories: 530, carbs: 93g, fat: 6g, fiber: 17g, Protein: 31g, sodium: 292mg

## Spinach and Sweet Pepper Poppers

Preparation time: 10 minutes, Cooking time: 8 minutes, Makes: 16 poppers

Ingredients:
- ½ tsp. of garlic powder
- 1 cup of fresh spinach leaves (chopped)
- 4 oz. (113 g) of cream cheese (softened)
- 8 mini sweet bell peppers (tops removed, seeded, & halved lengthwise)

Preparation:

1.    Mix the cream cheese, garlic powder, and spinach inside a medium bowl. Put 1 tbsp. mixture into each of the sweet pepper half then press it down to smoothen.

2.    Place the poppers into an ungreased air fryer basket. Then adjust the temperature to 400ºF or 204ºC and air fry it for 8 minutes. The poppers will be done as soon as the top of the cheese is browned and the peppers become tender and crisp.

3.    Serve warm.

**Nutritional Information per Serving:**
Calories: 31, carbs: 3g, fat: 2g, fiber: 0g, Protein: 1g, sodium: 34mg

## *Sweet and Crispy Roasted Pearl Onions*

Preparation time: 5 minutes, Cooking time: 18 minutes, Serves: 3

Ingredients:
- ¼ tsp. of black pepper
- ½ tsp. of kosher salt
- 1 (14½-oz. / 411-g) package of frozen pearl onions (don't thaw)
- 2 tbsps. of balsamic vinegar
- 2 tbsps. of extra-virgin olive oil
- 2 tsps. of fresh rosemary (finely chopped)

Preparation:
1.    Mix the onions, vinegar, olive oil, rosemary, pepper, and salt inside a medium bowl until well coated.

2.    Put the onions in the air fryer basket. Then set the air fryer to 400ºF or 204ºC for about 18 minutes, stirring one or two times while cooking until the onions become tender and a little charred.

**Nutritional Information per Serving:**
Calories: 145, carbs: 15g, fat: 9g, fiber: 2g, Protein: 2g, sodium: 396mg

# Five-Spice Roasted Sweet Potatoes

Preparation time: 10 minutes, Cooking time: 12 minutes, Serves: 4

Ingredients:
- ⅛ tsp. of turmeric
- ¼ tsp. of ground cumin
- ¼ tsp. of paprika
- ½ tsp. of ground cinnamon
- ½ tsp. of salt (optional)
- 1 tbsp. of olive oil
- 1 tsp. of chile powder
- 2 large sweet potatoes; peeled & cut into ¾" cubes (approximately 3 cups)
- Freshly ground black pepper (to taste)

Preparation:
1.   Mix the cinnamon, paprika, cumin, chile powder, salt, turmeric, and pepper (to taste) inside a big bowl.

2.   A, the potatoes stir very well.

3.   Drizzle the olive oil over the seasoned potatoes and stir well to coat evenly.

4.   Place the seasoned potatoes inside a baking pan or an ovenproof dish that fits right inside the air fryer basket.

5.   Cook at 390ºF or 199ºC for 6 minutes, then stop and stir very well.

6.   Cook for 6 minutes more.

**Nutritional Information per Serving:**
Calories: 14, carbs: 14g, fat: 3g, fiber: 2g, Protein: 1g, sodium: 327mg

# CHAPTER FIFTEEN

# VEGETARIAN MAINS

## *Crispy Eggplant Rounds*

Preparation time: 15 minutes, Cooking time: 10 minutes, Serves: 4

Ingredients:
- ¼ tsp. of garlic powder
- ½ tsp. of paprika
- ½ tsp. of salt
- 1 large egg
- 1 large eggplant (with the ends trimmed & cut into ½" slices)
- 2 oz. (57 g) of Parmesan 100% cheese crisps (finely ground)

Preparation:
1.    Sprinkle salt over the eggplant rounds then place the rounds on top of a kitchen towel for about 30 minutes to drain the excess water. Pat the rounds dry.

2.    Mix the garlic powder, paprika, and cheese crisps inside a medium bowl.

3.    Whisk the egg in a separate medium-sized bowl. Dip every one of the eggplant rounds inside the egg, then press it gently into the cheese crisps so that both sides coat well.

4.    Place the eggplant rounds in an ungreased air fryer basket. Then adjust the temp. to 400ºF or 204ºC and air fry it for 10 minutes; halfway through the cooking, turn the rounds. The eggplant will become golden and crispy after it is done.

5.    Serve warm.

**Nutritional Information per Serving:**
Calories: 113, carbs: 10g, fat: 5g, fiber: 4g, Protein: 7g, sodium: 567mg

# Stuffed Portobellos

Preparation time: 10 minutes, Cooking time: 8 minutes, Serves: 4

Ingredients:
- ¼ cup of red bell pepper (seeded & chopped)
- ½ medium zucchini (trimmed & chopped)
- ½ tsp. of salt
- 1½ cups of fresh spinach leaves (chopped)
- 2 tbsps. of coconut oil (melted)
- 3 oz. (85 g) of cream cheese (softened)
- 4 large portobello mushrooms (stems removed)

Preparation:
1.    Mix the cream cheese, spinach, pepper, and zucchini inside a medium bowl.

2.    Drizzle the coconut oil over the mushrooms and sprinkle with the salt. Then scoop ¼ of the zucchini mixture into each mushroom.

3.    Place the mushrooms in an ungreased air fryer basket. Then adjust the temp. to 400ºF or 204ºC and air fry for up to 8 minutes. The portobellos will get tender and their tops will get browned when it is done.

4.    Serve warm.

**Nutritional Information per Serving:**
Calories: 151, carbs: 6g, fat: 13g, fiber: 2g, Protein: 4g, sodium: 427mg

## Pistachio Mint Pesto Pasta

Preparation time: 10 minutes, Cooking time: 10 minutes, Serves: 4

Ingredients:
- ½ cup of fresh basil
- ½ tsp. of kosher salt
- 1 cup of fresh mint
- 1 garlic clove (peeled)
- $1/3$ cup of extra-virgin olive oil
- $1/3$ cup of unsalted pistachios (shelled)
- 8 oz. (227 g) of whole-wheat pasta
- Juice of ½ lime

Preparation:
1. Follow the package directions to cook the pasta. Drain but reserve ½ the cup of pasta water, then set it aside.

2. Put the mint, pistachios, basil, garlic, lime juice, and salt inside a food processor. Process it until the pistachios become coarsely ground. Then add the olive oil slowly and steadily and process it until incorporated.

3. Mix the pasta with the pistachio pesto inside a big bowl; toss properly to incorporate. But If you prefer a thinner and more saucy consistency, pour in some reserved pasta water then toss well.

**Nutritional Information per Serving:**
Calories: 420, carbs: 48g, fat: 3g, fiber: 2g, Protein: 11g, sodium: 150mg

## Moroccan Red Lentil and Pumpkin Stew

Preparation time: 10 minutes, Cooking time: 30 minutes, Serves: 4

Ingredients:
- ¼ cup of chopped cilantro (for garnish)
- 1 large onion (diced)
- 1 lb. (454 g) of pumpkin (peeled, seeded, & cut into 1" dice)
- 1 red bell pepper (seeded & diced)
- 1 tbsp. of curry powder
- 1 tsp. of ground cumin
- 1 tsp. of ground turmeric
- 1 tsp. of salt
- 1½ cups of red lentils (rinsed)
- 2 tbsps. of fresh ginger (minced)
- 2 tbsps. of olive oil
- 4 cloves garlic (minced)
- 6 cups of vegetable broth

Preparation:

1.    Heat the olive oil inside a stockpot placed over medium heat.

2.    Add the cumin, curry powder, and turmeric then cook for 1 minute, stirring, until fragrant. Add the salt and onion then cook for about 5 minutes, stirring often, until it softens. Add the garlic and ginger then cook for an additional 2 minutes, stirring often. Stir in the bell pepper and pumpkin, then add the broth and lentils, and bring it to a boil.

3.    Decrease the heat to a low and then simmer for approximately 20 minutes, uncovered, till the lentils become very tender.

4.    Garnished with the cilantro and serve hot.

**Nutritional Information per Serving:**

Calories: 405, carbs: 66g, fat: 9g, fiber: 11g, Protein: 20g, sodium: 594mg

# Stuffed Pepper Stew

Preparation time: 20 minutes, Cooking time: 50 minutes, Serves: 2

Ingredients:

- ¼ cup of brown lentils
- ¼ cup of brown rice
- ½ large onion  (minced)
- 1 cup of vegetable stock (low-sodium)
- 1 cup tomato juice (low-sodium)
- 1 garlic clove (minced)
- 1 tbsp. of gluten-free vegetarian Worcestershire sauce
- 1 tsp. of oregano
- 2 sweet peppers (diced, approximately 2 cups)
- 2 tbsps. of olive oil
- Salt

Preparation:

1.     Heat the olive oil inside a Dutch oven placed over medium-high heat. Add the onion and sweet peppers and sauté for about 10 minutes, or till the onion begins to turn golden and the peppers wilt.

2.     Add the Worcestershire sauce, garlic, and oregano, and cook for an additional 30 seconds. Then add the rice, tomato juice, vegetable stock, and lentils.

3.     Let the mixture boil. Cover it and decrease to medium-low heat. Simmer for about 45 minutes, or just until the rice cook and the lentils soften.

4.     Season with salt.

**Nutritional Information per Serving:**
Calories: 379, carbs: 53g, fat: 16g, fiber: 7g, Protein: 11g, sodium: 392mg

## Mozzarella and Sun-Dried Portobello Mushroom Pizza

Preparation time: 10 minutes, Cooking time: 10 minutes, Serves: 4

Ingredients:
- ½ - ¾ cup of tomato sauce (low-sodium)
- 1 cup of mozzarella cheese (divided)
- 3 tbsps. of extra-virgin olive oil
- 4 large portobello mushroom caps
- 4 sun-dried tomatoes
- Black pepper (freshly ground)
- Salt

Preparation:
1. Let the broiler preheat on high.

2. Drizzle olive oil over the mushroom caps on a baking sheet, then season with pepper and salt. Let each side of the portobello mushrooms broil for 5 minutes until tender, tossing once.

3. Fill each of the mushroom caps with 2 tbsps. of cheese, 1 sun-dried tomato, and 2-3 tbsps. of sauce. Top each one with 2 tbsps. of cheese.

4. Then put the caps back right under the broiler for another 2-3 minutes.

5. Quarter the mushrooms then serve.

**Nutritional Information per Serving:**
Calories: 218, carbs: 12g, fat: 16g, fiber: 2g, Protein: 11g, sodium: 244mg

## Freekeh, Chickpea, and Herb Salad

Preparation time: 15 minutes, Cooking time: 10 minutes, Serves: 4-6

Ingredients:
- 1 (15-ounce / 425-g) can of chickpeas, rinsed and drained
- 1 cup cooked freekeh
- 1 cup thinly sliced celery
- 1 bunch of scallions, both white and green parts, finely chopped
- ½ cup chopped fresh flat-leaf parsley
- ¼ cup chopped fresh mint
- 3 tablespoons chopped celery leaves
- ½ teaspoon kosher salt
- ⅓ cup extra-virgin olive oil
- ¼ cup freshly squeezed lemon juice
- ¼ teaspoon cumin seeds
- 1 teaspoon garlic powder

Preparation:
1. Mix the chickpeas, celery, freekeh, scallions, celery leaves, parsley, salt, and mint inside a big bowl, then toss lightly.

2. Whisk the cumin seeds, olive oil, garlic powder, and lemon juice together inside a small bowl. Once they are combined, add to the freekeh salad.

**Nutritional Information per Serving:**
Calories: 350, carbs: 38g, fat: 19g, fiber: 9g, Protein: 9g, sodium: 329mg

## *Quinoa with Almonds and Cranberries*

Preparation time: 15 minutes, Cooking time: 0 minutes, Serves: 4

Ingredients:
- ¼ cup of sliced almonds
- ¼ tsp. of black pepper (freshly ground)
- ¼ tsp. of ground cinnamon
- ⅓ tsp. of currants or cranberries
- ½ tsp. of ground cumin
- ½ tsp. of turmeric
- 1¼ tsps. of salt
- 2 cups of cooked quinoa
- 2 garlic cloves (minced)

Preparation:

1.    Toss the cranberries, quinoa, almonds, turmeric, garlic, salt, cumin, pepper, and cinnamon inside a big bowl, then stir to combine.

2.    Enjoy it alone or with the roasted cauliflower.

**Nutritional Information per Serving:**
Calories: 194, carbs: 31g, fat: 6g, fiber: 4g, Protein: 7g, sodium: 727mg

## *Herbed Ricotta–Stuffed Mushrooms*

Preparation time: 10 minutes, Cooking time: 30 minutes, Serves: 4

Ingredients:
- ¼ tsp. of black pepper (freshly ground)
- ⅓ cup of chopped fresh herbs (such as parsley, basil, rosemary, thyme, or oregano)

- ½ tsp. of salt
- 1 cup of whole-milk ricotta cheese
- 2 garlic cloves (finely minced)
- 4 portobello mushroom caps (cleaned & gills removed)
- 6 tbsps. of extra-virgin olive oil (divided)

Preparation:
1.    Let the oven preheat to 400°F or 205°C.

2.    Use foil or parchment to line a baking sheet and drizzle 2 tbsps. of olive oil over it, spreading it evenly. Keep the mushroom caps with their gill-side up over the baking sheet.

3.    Mix the herbs, ricotta, and 2 tbsps. of olive oil, garlic, pepper, and salt together inside a medium bowl. Then stuff each of the mushroom caps with ¼ of the cheese mixture, and, if needed, press it down.

4.    Drizzle with the leftover 2 tbsps. of olive oil then bake for 30-35 minutes until the mushrooms soften and turn a golden brown, depending on the mushrooms' size.

**Nutritional Information per Serving:**
Calories: 308, carbs: 6g, fat: 29g, fiber: 1g, Protein: 9g, sodium: 351mg

## Tangy Asparagus and Broccoli

Preparation time: 25 minutes, Cooking time: 22 minutes, Serves: 4

Ingredients:
- ½ cup of vegetable broth
- ½ lb. (227 g) of asparagus (cut into 1½" pieces)
- ½ lb. (227 g) of broccoli (cut into 1½" pieces)
- 2 tbsps. of apple cider vinegar
- 2 tbsps. of olive oil
- Salt (to taste)
- White pepper (to taste)

Preparation:

1.    Put the veggies in a single layer inside the lightly-greased air fryer basket. Then drizzle the vegetables with olive oil.

2.    Sprinkle with white pepper and salt.

3.    Cook for 15 minutes at 380ºF or 193ºC; halfway through the cooking time, shake the basket.

4.    Put ½ cup of the vegetable broth in a saucepan and bring it to a rapid boil then add the vinegar. Let it cook for 5-7 minutes or just until the sauce is reduced by half.

5.    Spoon the sauce on the warm veggies.

6.    Serve immediately.

**Nutritional Information per Serving:**
Calories: 93, carbs: 6g, fat: 7g, fiber: 3g, Protein: 3g, sodium: 89mg

# 175 DAYS (25 WEEKS) MEDITERRANEAN DIET MEAL PLAN

| Days | Breakfast | Lunch | Dinner | Snack/Dessert |
|---|---|---|---|---|
| 1 | Avocado Toast with Smoked Trout | Tomato Rice | Pork and Cabbage Egg Roll in a Bowl | Ricotta Cheesecake |
| 2 | Almond Butter Banana Chocolate Smoothie | Italian Halibut with Grapes and Olive Oil | Pasta Salad with Tomato, Arugula, & Feta | Figs with Mascarpone and Honey |
| 3 | Fig and Ricotta Toast with Walnuts and Honey | Sweet Potato and Chickpea Moroccan Stew | Spaghetti with Meaty Mushroom Sauce | Honey Ricotta with Espresso and Chocolate Chips |
| 4 | Berry Warming Smoothie | Mussels with Tomatoes and Herbs | Bowtie Pesto Pasta Salad | Strawberry-Pomegranate Molasses Sauce |
| 5 | Mediterranean-Inspired White Smoothie | Lentil & Zucchini Boats | Ground Pork and Eggplant Casserole | Greek Yogurt Ricotta Mousse |

| | | | | |
|---|---|---|---|---|
| 6 | Mediterranean Muesli and Breakfast Bowl | Za'atar Chicken Tenders | Couscous with Crab & Lemon | Ricotta with Balsamic Cherries & Black Pepper |
| 7 | Smoked Salmon Egg Scramble with Dill and Chives | Creamy Yellow Lentil Soup | Mediterranean Pork with Olives | Whipped Greek Yogurt with Chocolate |
| 8 | Black Olive Toast with Herbed Hummus | Baked Grouper with Tomatoes & Garlic | Pasta with Marinated Artichokes and Spinach | Greek Yogurt with Honey and Pomegranates |
| 9 | Breakfast Quinoa with Figs & Walnuts | Brown Rice with Apricots, Cherries, and Toasted Pecans | Moroccan Lamb Roast | Slow-Cooked Fruit Medley |
| 10 | Savory Cottage Cheese Breakfast Bowl | Shrimp with Marinara Sauce | Spaghetti with Fresh Mint Pesto and Ricotta Salata | Pears with Blue Cheese and Walnuts |
| 11 | Avocado Toast with | Moroccan Vegetables | Flank Steak and Blue | Sweet Potato Hummus |

|  |  |  |  |  |
|---|---|---|---|---|
|  | Smoked Trout | & Chickpeas | Cheese Wraps |  |
| 12 | Almond Butter Banana Chocolate Smoothie | Sea Bass with Roasted Root Vegetables | Harissa Yogurt Chicken Thighs | Roasted Rosemary Olives |
| 13 | Fig and Ricotta Toast with Walnuts and Honey | Baked Farro Risotto with Sage | Herb-Roasted Beef Tips with Onions | Baked Eggplant Baba Ganoush |
| 14 | Berry Warming Smoothie | Whitefish with Lemon and Capers | Greek Chicken Pasta Casserole | Warm Olives with Rosemary and Garlic |
| 15 | Mediterranea n-Inspired White Smoothie | Savory Gigantes Plaki (Baked Giant White Beans) | Garlic Balsamic London Broil | Seared Halloumi with Pesto and Tomato |
| 16 | Mediterranea n Muesli and Breakfast Bowl | Parmesan Mackerel with Coriander | Spicy Broccoli Pasta Salad | Lemony Olives and Feta Medley |
| 17 | Smoked Salmon Egg Scramble with Dill and Chives | Greek Baked Beans | Mediterranea n Beef Steaks | Creamy Traditional Hummus |

| | | | |
|---|---|---|---|
| 18 | Black Olive Toast with Herbed Hummus | Avgolemono | Turkey Burgers with Feta and Dill | Honey-Rosemary Almonds |
| 19 | Breakfast Quinoa with Figs & Walnuts | Spanish Rice | Flounder with Tomatoes and Basil | Taste of the Mediterranean Fat Bombs |
| 20 | Savory Cottage Cheese Breakfast Bowl | Tahini Soup | Turkey Breast in Yogurt Sauce | Salmon-Stuffed Cucumbers |
| 21 | Avocado Toast with Smoked Trout | Herb-Marinated Grilled Lamb Loin Chops | Citrus–Marinated Scallops | Ricotta Cheesecake |
| 22 | Smoked Salmon Egg Scramble with Dill and Chives | Tomato Rice | Pork and Cabbage Egg Roll in a Bowl | Ricotta Cheesecake |
| 23 | Breakfast Quinoa with Figs & Walnuts | Italian Halibut with Grapes and Olive Oil | Pasta Salad with Tomato, Arugula, & Feta | Figs with Mascarpone and Honey |

| | | | | |
|---|---|---|---|---|
| 24 | Savory Cottage Cheese Breakfast Bowl | Sweet Potato and Chickpea Moroccan Stew | Spaghetti with Meaty Mushroom Sauce | Honey Ricotta with Espresso and Chocolate Chips |
| 25 | Avocado Toast with Smoked Trout | Mussels with Tomatoes and Herbs | Bowtie Pesto Pasta Salad | Strawberry-Pomegranate Molasses Sauce |
| 26 | Smoked Salmon Egg Scramble with Dill and Chives | Lentil & Zucchini Boats | Ground Pork and Eggplant Casserole | Greek Yogurt Ricotta Mousse |
| 27 | Black Olive Toast with Herbed Hummus | Sea Bass with Roasted Root Vegetables | Couscous with Crab & Lemon | Ricotta with Balsamic Cherries & Black Pepper |
| 28 | Savory Cottage Cheese Breakfast Bowl | Baked Farro Risotto with Sage | Mediterranean Pork with Olives | Whipped Greek Yogurt with Chocolate |
| 29 | Breakfast Quinoa with Figs & Walnuts | Whitefish with Lemon and Capers | Pasta with Marinated Artichokes and Spinach | Greek Yogurt with Honey and Pomegranates |

| | | | |
|---|---|---|---|
| 30 | Black Olive Toast with Herbed Hummus | Savory Gigantes Plaki (Baked Giant White Beans) | Moroccan Lamb Roast | Slow-Cooked Fruit Medley |
| 31 | Avocado Toast with Smoked Trout | Parmesan Mackerel with Coriander | Spaghetti with Fresh Mint Pesto and Ricotta Salata | Pears with Blue Cheese and Walnuts |
| 32 | Smoked Salmon Egg Scramble with Dill and Chives | Greek Baked Beans | Flank Steak and Blue Cheese Wraps | Sweet Potato Hummus |
| 33 | Almond Butter Banana Chocolate Smoothie | Avgolemono | Harissa Yogurt Chicken Thighs | Roasted Rosemary Olives |
| 34 | Savory Cottage Cheese Breakfast Bowl | Creamy Yellow Lentil Soup | Herb-Roasted Beef Tips with Onions | Baked Eggplant Baba Ganoush |
| 35 | Black Olive Toast with | Baked Grouper with | Mediterranean Pork with Olives | Warm Olives with Rosemary and Garlic |

| | | | | |
|---|---|---|---|---|
| | Herbed Hummus | Tomatoes & Garlic | | |
| 36 | Breakfast Quinoa with Figs & Walnuts | Brown Rice with Apricots, Cherries, and Toasted Pecans | Pasta with Marinated Artichokes and Spinach | Seared Halloumi with Pesto and Tomato |
| 37 | Almond Butter Banana Chocolate Smoothie | Shrimp with Marinara Sauce | Moroccan Lamb Roast | Warm Olives with Rosemary and Garlic |
| 38 | Avocado Toast with Smoked Trout | Moroccan Vegetables & Chickpeas | Spaghetti with Fresh Mint Pesto and Ricotta Salata | Seared Halloumi with Pesto and Tomato |
| 39 | Smoked Salmon Egg Scramble with Dill and Chives | Sea Bass with Roasted Root Vegetables | Flank Steak and Blue Cheese Wraps | Lemony Olives and Feta Medley |
| 40 | Black Olive Toast with Herbed Hummus | Baked Farro Risotto with Sage | Harissa Yogurt Chicken Thighs | Creamy Traditional Hummus |

| | | | | |
|---|---|---|---|---|
| 41 | Savory Cottage Cheese Breakfast Bowl | Whitefish with Lemon and Capers | Herb-Roasted Beef Tips with Onions | Honey-Rosemary Almonds |
| 42 | Savory Cottage Cheese Breakfast Bowl | Savory Gigantes Plaki (Baked Giant White Beans) | Greek Chicken Pasta Casserole | Taste of the Mediterranean Fat Bombs |
| 43 | Almond Butter Banana Chocolate Smoothie | Za'atar Chicken Tenders | Garlic Balsamic London Broil | Salmon-Stuffed Cucumbers |
| 44 | Breakfast Quinoa with Figs & Walnuts | Creamy Yellow Lentil Soup | Spicy Broccoli Pasta Salad | Ricotta Cheesecake |
| 45 | Black Olive Toast with Herbed Hummus | Baked Grouper with Tomatoes & Garlic | Pork and Cabbage Egg Roll in a Bowl | Ricotta Cheesecake |
| 46 | Savory Cottage Cheese | Brown Rice with Apricots, Cherries, | Pasta Salad with Tomato, Arugula, & Feta | Figs with Mascarpone and Honey |

| | | | |
|---|---|---|---|
| | Breakfast Bowl | and Toasted Pecans | | |
| 47 | Breakfast Quinoa with Figs & Walnuts | Shrimp with Marinara Sauce | Spaghetti with Meaty Mushroom Sauce | Honey Ricotta with Espresso and Chocolate Chips |
| 48 | Almond Butter Banana Chocolate Smoothie | Moroccan Vegetables & Chickpeas | Bowtie Pesto Pasta Salad | Strawberry-Pomegranate Molasses Sauce |
| 49 | Avocado Toast with Smoked Trout | Sea Bass with Roasted Root Vegetables | Ground Pork and Eggplant Casserole | Greek Yogurt Ricotta Mousse |
| 50 | Smoked Salmon Egg Scramble with Dill and Chives | Creamy Yellow Lentil Soup | Couscous with Crab & Lemon | Ricotta with Balsamic Cherries & Black Pepper |
| 51 | Black Olive Toast with Herbed Hummus | Baked Grouper with Tomatoes & Garlic | Mediterranean Pork with Olives | Whipped Greek Yogurt with Chocolate |

| | | | | |
|---|---|---|---|---|
| 52 | Savory Cottage Cheese Breakfast Bowl | Brown Rice with Apricots, Cherries, and Toasted Pecans | Pasta with Marinated Artichokes and Spinach | Greek Yogurt with Honey and Pomegranates |
| 53 | Savory Cottage Cheese Breakfast Bowl | Shrimp with Marinara Sauce | Moroccan Lamb Roast | Ricotta Cheesecake |
| 54 | Breakfast Quinoa with Figs & Walnuts | Moroccan Vegetables & Chickpeas | Spaghetti with Fresh Mint Pesto and Ricotta Salata | Figs with Mascarpone and Honey |
| 55 | Almond Butter Banana Chocolate Smoothie | Sea Bass with Roasted Root Vegetables | Flank Steak and Blue Cheese Wraps | Honey Ricotta with Espresso and Chocolate Chips |
| 56 | Smoked Salmon Egg Scramble with Dill and Chives | Baked Farro Risotto with Sage | Harissa Yogurt Chicken Thighs | Strawberry-Pomegranate Molasses Sauce |

| | | | |
|---|---|---|---|
| 57 | Savory Cottage Cheese Breakfast Bowl | Whitefish with Lemon and Capers | Herb-Roasted Beef Tips with Onions | Greek Yogurt Ricotta Mousse |
| 58 | Avocado Toast with Smoked Trout | Savory Gigantes Plaki (Baked Giant White Beans) | Pork and Cabbage Egg Roll in a Bowl | Ricotta with Balsamic Cherries & Black Pepper |
| 59 | Breakfast Quinoa with Figs & Walnuts | Italian Halibut with Grapes and Olive Oil | Pasta Salad with Tomato, Arugula, & Feta | Whipped Greek Yogurt with Chocolate |
| 60 | Black Olive Toast with Herbed Hummus | Sweet Potato and Chickpea Moroccan Stew | Spaghetti with Meaty Mushroom Sauce | Greek Yogurt with Honey and Pomegranates |
| 61 | Savory Cottage Cheese Breakfast Bowl | Mussels with Tomatoes and Herbs | Bowtie Pesto Pasta Salad | Slow-Cooked Fruit Medley |
| 62 | Savory Cottage Cheese | Lentil & Zucchini Boats | Ground Pork and Eggplant Casserole | Pears with Blue Cheese and Walnuts |

| | | | |
|---|---|---|---|
| | Breakfast Bowl | | | |
| 63 | Smoked Salmon Egg Scramble with Dill and Chives | Za'atar Chicken Tenders | Couscous with Crab & Lemon | Sweet Potato Hummus |
| 64 | Almond Butter Banana Chocolate Smoothie | Creamy Yellow Lentil Soup | Mediterranean Pork with Olives | Roasted Rosemary Olives |
| 65 | Savory Cottage Cheese Breakfast Bowl | Baked Grouper with Tomatoes & Garlic | Pasta with Marinated Artichokes and Spinach | Baked Eggplant Baba Ganoush |
| 66 | Black Olive Toast with Herbed Hummus | Brown Rice with Apricots, Cherries, and Toasted Pecans | Moroccan Lamb Roast | Warm Olives with Rosemary and Garlic |
| 67 | Breakfast Quinoa with Figs & Walnuts | Shrimp with Marinara Sauce | Spaghetti with Fresh Mint Pesto and Ricotta Salata | Seared Halloumi with Pesto and Tomato |

| | | | | |
|---|---|---|---|---|
| 68 | Almond Butter Banana Chocolate Smoothie | Moroccan Vegetables & Chickpeas | Flank Steak and Blue Cheese Wraps | Slow-Cooked Fruit Medley |
| 69 | Avocado Toast with Smoked Trout | Sea Bass with Roasted Root Vegetables | Harissa Yogurt Chicken Thighs | Pears with Blue Cheese and Walnuts |
| 70 | Breakfast Quinoa with Figs & Walnuts | Baked Farro Risotto with Sage | Herb-Roasted Beef Tips with Onions | Sweet Potato Hummus |
| 71 | Savory Cottage Cheese Breakfast Bowl | Creamy Yellow Lentil Soup | Moroccan Lamb Roast | Roasted Rosemary Olives |
| 72 | Smoked Salmon Egg Scramble with Dill and Chives | Baked Grouper with Tomatoes & Garlic | Spaghetti with Fresh Mint Pesto and Ricotta Salata | Baked Eggplant Baba Ganoush |
| 73 | Avocado Toast with Smoked Trout | Tomato Rice | Pork and Cabbage Egg Roll in a Bowl | Ricotta Cheesecake |

| | | | |
|---|---|---|---|
| 74 | Almond Butter Banana Chocolate Smoothie | Italian Halibut with Grapes and Olive Oil | Pasta Salad with Tomato, Arugula, & Feta | Figs with Mascarpone and Honey |
| 75 | Fig and Ricotta Toast with Walnuts and Honey | Sweet Potato and Chickpea Moroccan Stew | Spaghetti with Meaty Mushroom Sauce | Honey Ricotta with Espresso and Chocolate Chips |
| 76 | Berry Warming Smoothie | Mussels with Tomatoes and Herbs | Bowtie Pesto Pasta Salad | Strawberry-Pomegranate Molasses Sauce |
| 77 | Mediterranean-Inspired White Smoothie | Lentil & Zucchini Boats | Ground Pork and Eggplant Casserole | Greek Yogurt Ricotta Mousse |
| 78 | Mediterranean Muesli and Breakfast Bowl | Za'atar Chicken Tenders | Couscous with Crab & Lemon | Ricotta with Balsamic Cherries & Black Pepper |
| 79 | Smoked Salmon Egg Scramble with Dill and Chives | Creamy Yellow Lentil Soup | Mediterranean Pork with Olives | Whipped Greek Yogurt with Chocolate |

| | | | | |
|---|---|---|---|---|
| 80 | Black Olive Toast with Herbed Hummus | Baked Grouper with Tomatoes & Garlic | Pasta with Marinated Artichokes and Spinach | Greek Yogurt with Honey and Pomegranates |
| 81 | Breakfast Quinoa with Figs & Walnuts | Brown Rice with Apricots, Cherries, and Toasted Pecans | Moroccan Lamb Roast | Slow-Cooked Fruit Medley |
| 82 | Savory Cottage Cheese Breakfast Bowl | Shrimp with Marinara Sauce | Spaghetti with Fresh Mint Pesto and Ricotta Salata | Pears with Blue Cheese and Walnuts |
| 83 | Avocado Toast with Smoked Trout | Moroccan Vegetables & Chickpeas | Flank Steak and Blue Cheese Wraps | Sweet Potato Hummus |
| 84 | Almond Butter Banana Chocolate Smoothie | Sea Bass with Roasted Root Vegetables | Harissa Yogurt Chicken Thighs | Roasted Rosemary Olives |
| 85 | Fig and Ricotta Toast | Baked Farro | Herb-Roasted Beef Tips with Onions | Baked Eggplant Baba Ganoush |

| | | | |
|---|---|---|---|
| | with Walnuts and Honey | Risotto with Sage | | |
| 86 | Berry Warming Smoothie | Whitefish with Lemon and Capers | Greek Chicken Pasta Casserole | Warm Olives with Rosemary and Garlic |
| 87 | Mediterranean-Inspired White Smoothie | Savory Gigantes Plaki (Baked Giant White Beans) | Garlic Balsamic London Broil | Seared Halloumi with Pesto and Tomato |
| 88 | Mediterranean Muesli and Breakfast Bowl | Parmesan Mackerel with Coriander | Spicy Broccoli Pasta Salad | Lemony Olives and Feta Medley |
| 89 | Smoked Salmon Egg Scramble with Dill and Chives | Greek Baked Beans | Mediterranean Beef Steaks | Creamy Traditional Hummus |
| 90 | Black Olive Toast with Herbed Hummus | Avgolemono | Turkey Burgers with Feta and Dill | Honey-Rosemary Almonds |
| 91 | Breakfast Quinoa with Figs & Walnuts | Spanish Rice | Flounder with Tomatoes and Basil | Taste of the Mediterranean Fat Bombs |

| | | | |
|---|---|---|---|
| 92 | Savory Cottage Cheese Breakfast Bowl | Tahini Soup | Turkey Breast in Yogurt Sauce | Salmon-Stuffed Cucumbers |
| 93 | Avocado Toast with Smoked Trout | Herb-Marinated Grilled Lamb Loin Chops | Citrus–Marinated Scallops | Ricotta Cheesecake |
| 94 | Smoked Salmon Egg Scramble with Dill and Chives | Tomato Rice | Pork and Cabbage Egg Roll in a Bowl | Ricotta Cheesecake |
| 95 | Breakfast Quinoa with Figs & Walnuts | Italian Halibut with Grapes and Olive Oil | Pasta Salad with Tomato, Arugula, & Feta | Figs with Mascarpone and Honey |
| 96 | Savory Cottage Cheese Breakfast Bowl | Sweet Potato and Chickpea Moroccan Stew | Spaghetti with Meaty Mushroom Sauce | Honey Ricotta with Espresso and Chocolate Chips |
| 97 | Avocado Toast with Smoked Trout | Mussels with Tomatoes and Herbs | Bowtie Pesto Pasta Salad | Strawberry-Pomegranate Molasses Sauce |

| | | | | |
|---|---|---|---|---|
| 98 | Smoked Salmon Egg Scramble with Dill and Chives | Lentil & Zucchini Boats | Ground Pork and Eggplant Casserole | Greek Yogurt Ricotta Mousse |
| 99 | Black Olive Toast with Herbed Hummus | Sea Bass with Roasted Root Vegetables | Couscous with Crab & Lemon | Ricotta with Balsamic Cherries & Black Pepper |
| 100 | Savory Cottage Cheese Breakfast Bowl | Baked Farro Risotto with Sage | Mediterranean Pork with Olives | Whipped Greek Yogurt with Chocolate |
| 101 | Breakfast Quinoa with Figs & Walnuts | Whitefish with Lemon and Capers | Pasta with Marinated Artichokes and Spinach | Greek Yogurt with Honey and Pomegranates |
| 102 | Black Olive Toast with Herbed Hummus | Savory Gigantes Plaki (Baked Giant White Beans) | Moroccan Lamb Roast | Slow-Cooked Fruit Medley |
| 103 | Avocado Toast with Smoked Trout | Parmesan Mackerel with Coriander | Spaghetti with Fresh Mint Pesto | Pears with Blue Cheese and Walnuts |

| | | | and Ricotta Salata | |
|---|---|---|---|---|
| 104 | Smoked Salmon Egg Scramble with Dill and Chives | Greek Baked Beans | Flank Steak and Blue Cheese Wraps | Sweet Potato Hummus |
| 105 | Almond Butter Banana Chocolate Smoothie | Avgolemono | Harissa Yogurt Chicken Thighs | Roasted Rosemary Olives |
| 106 | Savory Cottage Cheese Breakfast Bowl | Creamy Yellow Lentil Soup | Herb-Roasted Beef Tips with Onions | Baked Eggplant Baba Ganoush |
| 107 | Black Olive Toast with Herbed Hummus | Baked Grouper with Tomatoes & Garlic | Mediterranean Pork with Olives | Warm Olives with Rosemary and Garlic |
| 108 | Breakfast Quinoa with Figs & Walnuts | Brown Rice with Apricots, Cherries, and Toasted Pecans | Pasta with Marinated Artichokes and Spinach | Seared Halloumi with Pesto and Tomato |

| | | | |
|---|---|---|---|
| 109 | Almond Butter Banana Chocolate Smoothie | Shrimp with Marinara Sauce | Moroccan Lamb Roast | Warm Olives with Rosemary and Garlic |
| 110 | Avocado Toast with Smoked Trout | Moroccan Vegetables & Chickpeas | Spaghetti with Fresh Mint Pesto and Ricotta Salata | Seared Halloumi with Pesto and Tomato |
| 111 | Smoked Salmon Egg Scramble with Dill and Chives | Sea Bass with Roasted Root Vegetables | Flank Steak and Blue Cheese Wraps | Lemony Olives and Feta Medley |
| 112 | Black Olive Toast with Herbed Hummus | Baked Farro Risotto with Sage | Harissa Yogurt Chicken Thighs | Creamy Traditional Hummus |
| 113 | Savory Cottage Cheese Breakfast Bowl | Whitefish with Lemon and Capers | Herb-Roasted Beef Tips with Onions | Honey-Rosemary Almonds |
| 114 | Savory Cottage Cheese Breakfast Bowl | Savory Gigantes Plaki (Baked | Greek Chicken Pasta Casserole | Taste of the Mediterranean Fat Bombs |

| | | Giant White Beans) | | |
|---|---|---|---|---|
| 115 | Almond Butter Banana Chocolate Smoothie | Za'atar Chicken Tenders | Garlic Balsamic London Broil | Salmon-Stuffed Cucumbers |
| 116 | Breakfast Quinoa with Figs & Walnuts | Creamy Yellow Lentil Soup | Spicy Broccoli Pasta Salad | Ricotta Cheesecake |
| 117 | Black Olive Toast with Herbed Hummus | Baked Grouper with Tomatoes & Garlic | Pork and Cabbage Egg Roll in a Bowl | Ricotta Cheesecake |
| 118 | Savory Cottage Cheese Breakfast Bowl | Brown Rice with Apricots, Cherries, and Toasted Pecans | Pasta Salad with Tomato, Arugula, & Feta | Figs with Mascarpone and Honey |
| 119 | Breakfast Quinoa with Figs & Walnuts | Shrimp with Marinara Sauce | Spaghetti with Meaty Mushroom Sauce | Honey Ricotta with Espresso and Chocolate Chips |

| | | | |
|---|---|---|---|
| 120 | Almond Butter Banana Chocolate Smoothie | Moroccan Vegetables & Chickpeas | Bowtie Pesto Pasta Salad | Strawberry-Pomegranate Molasses Sauce |
| 121 | Avocado Toast with Smoked Trout | Sea Bass with Roasted Root Vegetables | Ground Pork and Eggplant Casserole | Greek Yogurt Ricotta Mousse |
| 122 | Smoked Salmon Egg Scramble with Dill and Chives | Creamy Yellow Lentil Soup | Couscous with Crab & Lemon | Ricotta with Balsamic Cherries & Black Pepper |
| 123 | Black Olive Toast with Herbed Hummus | Baked Grouper with Tomatoes & Garlic | Mediterranean Pork with Olives | Whipped Greek Yogurt with Chocolate |
| 124 | Savory Cottage Cheese Breakfast Bowl | Brown Rice with Apricots, Cherries, and Toasted Pecans | Pasta with Marinated Artichokes and Spinach | Greek Yogurt with Honey and Pomegranates |
| 125 | Savory Cottage | Shrimp with | Moroccan Lamb Roast | Ricotta Cheesecake |

| | | | |
|---|---|---|---|
| | Cheese Breakfast Bowl | Marinara Sauce | | |
| 126 | Breakfast Quinoa with Figs & Walnuts | Moroccan Vegetables & Chickpeas | Spaghetti with Fresh Mint Pesto and Ricotta Salata | Figs with Mascarpone and Honey |
| 127 | Almond Butter Banana Chocolate Smoothie | Sea Bass with Roasted Root Vegetables | Flank Steak and Blue Cheese Wraps | Honey Ricotta with Espresso and Chocolate Chips |
| 128 | Avocado Toast with Smoked Trout | Tomato Rice | Pork and Cabbage Egg Roll in a Bowl | Ricotta Cheesecake |
| 129 | Almond Butter Banana Chocolate Smoothie | Italian Halibut with Grapes and Olive Oil | Pasta Salad with Tomato, Arugula, & Feta | Figs with Mascarpone and Honey |
| 130 | Fig and Ricotta Toast with Walnuts and Honey | Sweet Potato and Chickpea Moroccan Stew | Spaghetti with Meaty Mushroom Sauce | Honey Ricotta with Espresso and Chocolate Chips |

| | | | |
|---|---|---|---|
| 131 | Berry Warming Smoothie | Mussels with Tomatoes and Herbs | Bowtie Pesto Pasta Salad | Strawberry-Pomegranate Molasses Sauce |
| 132 | Mediterranean-Inspired White Smoothie | Lentil & Zucchini Boats | Ground Pork and Eggplant Casserole | Greek Yogurt Ricotta Mousse |
| 133 | Mediterranean Muesli and Breakfast Bowl | Za'atar Chicken Tenders | Couscous with Crab & Lemon | Ricotta with Balsamic Cherries & Black Pepper |
| 134 | Smoked Salmon Egg Scramble with Dill and Chives | Creamy Yellow Lentil Soup | Mediterranean Pork with Olives | Whipped Greek Yogurt with Chocolate |
| 135 | Black Olive Toast with Herbed Hummus | Baked Grouper with Tomatoes & Garlic | Pasta with Marinated Artichokes and Spinach | Greek Yogurt with Honey and Pomegranates |
| 136 | Breakfast Quinoa with Figs & Walnuts | Brown Rice with Apricots, Cherries, and Toasted Pecans | Moroccan Lamb Roast | Slow-Cooked Fruit Medley |

| 137 | Savory Cottage Cheese Breakfast Bowl | Shrimp with Marinara Sauce | Spaghetti with Fresh Mint Pesto and Ricotta Salata | Pears with Blue Cheese and Walnuts |
|---|---|---|---|---|
| 138 | Avocado Toast with Smoked Trout | Moroccan Vegetables & Chickpeas | Flank Steak and Blue Cheese Wraps | Sweet Potato Hummus |
| 139 | Almond Butter Banana Chocolate Smoothie | Sea Bass with Roasted Root Vegetables | Harissa Yogurt Chicken Thighs | Roasted Rosemary Olives |
| 140 | Fig and Ricotta Toast with Walnuts and Honey | Baked Farro Risotto with Sage | Herb-Roasted Beef Tips with Onions | Baked Eggplant Baba Ganoush |
| 141 | Berry Warming Smoothie | Whitefish with Lemon and Capers | Greek Chicken Pasta Casserole | Warm Olives with Rosemary and Garlic |
| 142 | Mediterranean-Inspired White Smoothie | Savory Gigantes Plaki (Baked Giant White Beans) | Garlic Balsamic London Broil | Seared Halloumi with Pesto and Tomato |
| 143 | Mediterranean Muesli and | Parmesan Mackerel | Spicy Broccoli Pasta Salad | Lemony Olives and Feta Medley |

| | | | | |
|---|---|---|---|---|
| | Breakfast Bowl | with Coriander | | |
| 144 | Smoked Salmon Egg Scramble with Dill and Chives | Greek Baked Beans | Mediterranean Beef Steaks | Creamy Traditional Hummus |
| 145 | Black Olive Toast with Herbed Hummus | Avgolemono | Turkey Burgers with Feta and Dill | Honey-Rosemary Almonds |
| 146 | Breakfast Quinoa with Figs & Walnuts | Spanish Rice | Flounder with Tomatoes and Basil | Taste of the Mediterranean Fat Bombs |
| 147 | Savory Cottage Cheese Breakfast Bowl | Tahini Soup | Turkey Breast in Yogurt Sauce | Salmon-Stuffed Cucumbers |
| 148 | Avocado Toast with Smoked Trout | Herb-Marinated Grilled Lamb Loin Chops | Citrus–Marinated Scallops | Ricotta Cheesecake |
| 149 | Smoked Salmon Egg Scramble | Tomato Rice | Pork and Cabbage Egg Roll in a Bowl | Ricotta Cheesecake |

| | | | |
|---|---|---|---|
| | with Dill and Chives | | | |
| 150 | Breakfast Quinoa with Figs & Walnuts | Italian Halibut with Grapes and Olive Oil | Pasta Salad with Tomato, Arugula, & Feta | Figs with Mascarpone and Honey |
| 151 | Savory Cottage Cheese Breakfast Bowl | Sweet Potato and Chickpea Moroccan Stew | Spaghetti with Meaty Mushroom Sauce | Honey Ricotta with Espresso and Chocolate Chips |
| 152 | Avocado Toast with Smoked Trout | Mussels with Tomatoes and Herbs | Bowtie Pesto Pasta Salad | Strawberry-Pomegranate Molasses Sauce |
| 153 | Smoked Salmon Egg Scramble with Dill and Chives | Lentil & Zucchini Boats | Ground Pork and Eggplant Casserole | Greek Yogurt Ricotta Mousse |
| 154 | Black Olive Toast with Herbed Hummus | Sea Bass with Roasted Root Vegetables | Couscous with Crab & Lemon | Ricotta with Balsamic Cherries & Black Pepper |
| 155 | Savory Cottage Cheese | Baked Farro | Mediterranean Pork with Olives | Whipped Greek Yogurt with Chocolate |

|  | Breakfast Bowl | Risotto with Sage |  |  |
|---|---|---|---|---|
| 156 | Breakfast Quinoa with Figs & Walnuts | Whitefish with Lemon and Capers | Pasta with Marinated Artichokes and Spinach | Greek Yogurt with Honey and Pomegranates |
| 157 | Black Olive Toast with Herbed Hummus | Savory Gigantes Plaki (Baked Giant White Beans) | Moroccan Lamb Roast | Slow-Cooked Fruit Medley |
| 158 | Avocado Toast with Smoked Trout | Parmesan Mackerel with Coriander | Spaghetti with Fresh Mint Pesto and Ricotta Salata | Pears with Blue Cheese and Walnuts |
| 159 | Smoked Salmon Egg Scramble with Dill and Chives | Greek Baked Beans | Flank Steak and Blue Cheese Wraps | Sweet Potato Hummus |
| 160 | Almond Butter Banana Chocolate Smoothie | Avgolemono | Harissa Yogurt Chicken Thighs | Roasted Rosemary Olives |

| | | | | |
|---|---|---|---|---|
| 161 | Savory Cottage Cheese Breakfast Bowl | Creamy Yellow Lentil Soup | Herb-Roasted Beef Tips with Onions | Baked Eggplant Baba Ganoush |
| 162 | Black Olive Toast with Herbed Hummus | Baked Grouper with Tomatoes & Garlic | Mediterranean Pork with Olives | Warm Olives with Rosemary and Garlic |
| 163 | Breakfast Quinoa with Figs & Walnuts | Brown Rice with Apricots, Cherries, and Toasted Pecans | Pasta with Marinated Artichokes and Spinach | Seared Halloumi with Pesto and Tomato |
| 164 | Almond Butter Banana Chocolate Smoothie | Shrimp with Marinara Sauce | Moroccan Lamb Roast | Warm Olives with Rosemary and Garlic |
| 165 | Avocado Toast with Smoked Trout | Moroccan Vegetables & Chickpeas | Spaghetti with Fresh Mint Pesto and Ricotta Salata | Seared Halloumi with Pesto and Tomato |
| 166 | Smoked Salmon Egg | Sea Bass with | Flank Steak and Blue | Lemony Olives and Feta Medley |

|  | | | |
|---|---|---|---|
|  | Scramble with Dill and Chives | Roasted Root Vegetables | Cheese Wraps | |
| 167 | Black Olive Toast with Herbed Hummus | Baked Farro Risotto with Sage | Harissa Yogurt Chicken Thighs | Creamy Traditional Hummus |
| 168 | Savory Cottage Cheese Breakfast Bowl | Whitefish with Lemon and Capers | Herb-Roasted Beef Tips with Onions | Honey-Rosemary Almonds |
| 169 | Savory Cottage Cheese Breakfast Bowl | Savory Gigantes Plaki (Baked Giant White Beans) | Greek Chicken Pasta Casserole | Taste of the Mediterranean Fat Bombs |
| 170 | Almond Butter Banana Chocolate Smoothie | Za'atar Chicken Tenders | Garlic Balsamic London Broil | Salmon-Stuffed Cucumbers |
| 171 | Breakfast Quinoa with Figs & Walnuts | Creamy Yellow Lentil Soup | Spicy Broccoli Pasta Salad | Ricotta Cheesecake |

| | | | |
|---|---|---|---|
| 172 | Black Olive Toast with Herbed Hummus | Baked Grouper with Tomatoes & Garlic | Pork and Cabbage Egg Roll in a Bowl | Ricotta Cheesecake |
| 173 | Savory Cottage Cheese Breakfast Bowl | Brown Rice with Apricots, Cherries, and Toasted Pecans | Pasta Salad with Tomato, Arugula, & Feta | Figs with Mascarpone and Honey |
| 174 | Breakfast Quinoa with Figs & Walnuts | Shrimp with Marinara Sauce | Spaghetti with Meaty Mushroom Sauce | Honey Ricotta with Espresso and Chocolate Chips |
| 175 | Almond Butter Banana Chocolate Smoothie | Moroccan Vegetables & Chickpeas | Bowtie Pesto Pasta Salad | Strawberry-Pomegranate Molasses Sauce |

# CONCLUSION

The Mediterranean diet is not only delicious but also a healthy way to eat. The diet is based on the traditional foods people eat in countries like Italy and Greece. These countries have some of the lowest rates of heart disease and obesity. The Mediterranean diet also improves blood pressure, cholesterol levels, and overall health.

So, if you want a delicious and healthy way to eat, the Mediterranean diet is a great option.

www.ingramcontent.com/pod-product-compliance
Lightning Source LLC
Chambersburg PA
CBHW081326120626
46546CB00011B/3241